RETIRE

YOUR FEAR,

PLAN

YOUR FUTURE

KELLY KELLY

Kelly Kelly /Kelly Financial Services LLC
10 Forbes, Suite 130, Braintree, MA 02184
kellyfinancial.org

Book layout ©2022 Advisors Excel, LLC

Retire Your Fear, Plan Your Future/Kelly Kelly. — 1st edition

ISBN 9798370045363

Kelly Kelly is a licensed insurance agent in the states of Massachusetts, Rhode Island, New Hampshire, Connecticut, Florida, and Arizona. Kelly Financial Services LLC is an independent financial services firm that helps individuals create retirement strategies using a variety of investment and insurance products to custom suit their needs and objectives.

The contents of this book are provided for informational purposes only and are not intended to serve as the basis for any financial decisions. Any tax, legal, or estate planning information is general in nature. It should not be construed as legal or tax advice. Always consult an attorney or tax professional regarding the applicability of this information to your unique situation.

Information presented is believed to be factual and up to date, but we do not guarantee its accuracy, and it should not be regarded as a complete analysis of the subjects discussed. All expressions of opinion are those of the author as of the date of publication and are subject to change. Content should not be construed as personalized investment advice, nor should it be interpreted as an offer to buy or sell any securities mentioned. A financial advisor should be consulted before implementing any of the strategies presented.

Investing involves risk, including the potential loss of principal. No investment strategy can guarantee a profit or protect against loss in periods of declining values. Any references to protection benefits or guaranteed/lifetime income streams refer only to fixed insurance products, not securities or investment products. Insurance and annuity product guarantees are backed by the financial strength and claims-paying ability of the issuing insurance company.

Any names used in the examples in this book are hypothetical only and do not represent actual clients.

"Plan ahead: It wasn't raining when Noah built the ark."

~ Richard Cardinal Cushing

Dedicated to the memory of my dear late husband and business partner, Bill Kelly.

And everyone who stood with me and continues to stand with me today. You know who you are.

"Life is good," Bill Kelly always said.

Table of Contents

The Importance of Planning

T he irony was lost on me.

On a crisp autumn day, my husband, a vibrant Irish Catholic, was being laid to rest on All Hallows' Eve, the beginning of what Western Christians refer to as Allhallowtide—the season encompassing the triduum of All Saints' Eve, All Saints' Day, and All Souls' Day. Well after the funeral, admittedly, it took me some time to appreciate the idea that Allhallowtide is a time to remember the dead, including martyrs, saints, and all faithful departed Christians.

Since then, out of a sense of curiosity and search for higher meaning, I have read that many Halloween traditions were influenced by Celtic harvest festivals. In so many ways, in retrospect, this was befitting of the way my husband left this world. Life moves in cycles. All aspects of his life were about continuous planning, planting, and harvesting—in faith, in family, and in vocation. I realized that he was being called home to the ultimate harvest. That thought comforts me today.

Still, I was jolted by this harsh reality: In a flash, I became a widow, a single mom, a client, and a CEO, all on the same day. Life can and does change unexpectedly.

Bill Kelly died tragically on October 15, 2017, at the age of sixty-five, semi-retired, yet fulfilled by life's promise and yes, its peril, too. He passed while our family was in the Dominican Republic. Our son, William Jr., was with his father during his last living moments (he literally died in our arms); our daughter, Mary Madeline, was at school. Both were very close to their father.

Bill was the public face and force of our family-owned business, a business we built together, beginning in the early 2000s. He was a financial advisor, radio host, author, philanthropist, and co-founder of what became Kelly Financial Services LLC. Those were his professional occupations. He was also—and perhaps most importantly—a husband, father, brother, uncle, son, mentor, and friend, among other roles, in his private life. He cherished and relished all of them. He lived a blessed life: he knew it, talked about it, and reciprocated it. But none of this was guaranteed.

We came from very different places. I grew up in the south—Valdosta, Georgia. Bill was 100 percent New England Yankee, born and raised in Newport, Rhode Island. And our personalities were about as far apart as a country mile. But, as is said, opposites attract. We met by virtue of a tennis challenge, despite our 10-year age difference.

There were plenty of similarities, especially in our backgrounds. We both grew up on or near farms. We both had come from a long lineage of entrepreneurs. And we shared a deeply held belief in the importance of family, friends, and faith as the sinews of personal development and growth. To me, these are the building blocks of our rich culture and tradition. And makes us, well ... us.

Bill lived a hardscrabble life growing up. I am convinced that the lessons of hardship during his formative years greatly impacted him and served him well later on—chiefly his sense of empathy for others who were less fortunate. Much his family's wealth was lost during the Great Depression. Despite all of this, he was happy and always believed that things would get better—he was a quiet optimist.

He graduated from Middletown High School in 1970, where he was a National Merit Scholar. While attending the University of Rhode Island, he served in the U.S. Army National Guard and was honorably discharged in 1975. He later enlisted in the U.S. Air Force, where he served another four years as an avionics engineer, pioneering computer guidance systems for the F-15 jet fighter.

Bill continued his engineering work with the Bendix Aerospace Corporation. In 1984, he founded computer software company Viking Technologies, exercising the formidable leadership and business skills he subsequently would need in the financial services industry.

I began involvement in business early on. By age fifteen, I was already doing accounting work for my family's John Deere dealership. (My dad, now in his eighties, is still on the farm, full of vim and vigor, advice, and agriculture.)

Not far from home, I earned a bachelor's degree in business administration from Valdosta State University. I worked for a large marketing services firm in Atlanta, Georgia, that specialized in financial institutions. I also founded and ran a successful gourmet specialty food business with my mother for more than 10 years. That kept me exploring and traveling the country.

Sometime in the 1990s, Bill wanted to get into the financial services business. It was a bit of a gamble as he was starting from nothing and starting on his own. But it was also not surprising. He was the classic Baby Boomer entrepreneur.

Bill was motivated by the fact that he could impart objective and sensible financial advice to people if only because he too witnessed and experienced the very challenges people face every day. He worked in the private sector and the government. He faced financial hardships in his life. He understood what made people tick (people wanted to live a comfortable retirement and leave some behind for their families). And Bill had a calling—his religious and spiritual beliefs guided him. Really, he was inspired to help people.

And so began our journey together.

We had a vision. We envisioned a financial services company built upon, and dedicated to, a simple but powerful concept: family values combined with financial knowledge. That was our core philosophy in how we served people. It may sound hokey to the likes of so-called sophisticated, big-wheel financial types. But Bill and I knew instinctively that everyday people needed and deserved sound financial advice and support, too.

I confess that it was a real struggle at first. We risked a lot. We saved and used our personal assets to build the business. Everything in our lives was dedicated to growing our company. I wouldn't be human if I didn't sometimes wonder whether all the sacrifice was worth it during the first few years.

The response from those who became clients (many of those earliest clients are still clients today) was overwhelming. Relief, for sure, the connection we made was humbling and heartwarming. It was as if they felt they were ignored by the big financial institutions. Either they didn't have the minimum asset levels, or their potential asset growth was deemed to be too slow to work with these big firms. These everyday people felt like they had a place to go to. They could relate to Bill and our philosophy. We began to feel that we were serving the underserved.

We had a plan.

Planning is critical in our business. It is important to have one—in your professional life and in your private life. Yes, plans can and do change. That's expected.

Everyone should have a plan. That said, I know your plan will be different from someone else's. Let me take a moment to share with you how we devised plans for our company and our personal circumstances.

Like many before him, Bill began helping clients with their insurance needs. Soon, though, he wanted to offer clients asset management and address legacy needs, like trust and estate planning, as well. It was a nod to a more holistic approach to advising clients and their ever-growing needs. He devised a growth plan.

He built the marketing and advisory side of things (for example, in-person events, a radio show, books, quarterly meetings with clients). I focused on the operations (call center, logistics). Together, we added staffing and two more office locations, and we expanded our brand.

The emphasis centered around planning. How often do you ask yourself or others, "What's your plan?" It's a common question and grabs your attention.

Part of our role is that of financial planners. That said, we formalize planning. When we work with clients, we actually start with setting goals. From there, we help clients formulate a plan to achieve those goals. But as I mentioned earlier, plans (along with goals) have a way of going awry. They change. So how do we build plans that have enough flexibility yet still focus on goals? We put into place a process.

Our process, now known as "Safe Money Strategies,™" keeps planning in check. By using a process, our clients have a better chance of reaching their goals, than if they were not to use a process. A process is helpful in that it also aids our advisors. By following a process, they will be in a better position to help our clients identify when plans may need to be altered. All of this is done continuously. It all serves one thing: achieving your goals.

Business was good. Our plans for growth coincided with baby boomers who were retiring in record numbers (10,000 a day). I think the key was that we also tapped into people's sense of values. Sharing the same values is the foundation of what makes truly long-term relationships.

We wouldn't be true to our word if we didn't practice what we preached. Bill and I were semi-retired when he died. But we planned in advance should something happen to either of us to ensure that our business continued and that our clients would be served. We shored up our personal affairs, too.

I appreciate the reluctance of people not wanting to address sensitive, personal matters, like planning for the death of a loved one—particularly when everything seems to be going well and people are in relatively good health. It is depressing, and it can be complicated. But we all know friends and family members who ultimately regret not having put the time and commitment to a plan after the unthinkable happens.

The unthinkable happened to me, my family, and our business.

Kelly Financial Services exists today because we planned for the very event no one thought would ever happen: one of us dying (I always thought Bill would outlive me). We were able to continue serving our clients because we worked on succession planning. I was able to continue living and providing a desired lifestyle for my kids because we worked on personal planning. But I would be lying to you if I said it was easy. It was very difficult and painful. Grieving would come later.

In those first hours after Bill passed, I mobilized our team. They responded with courage, poise, and professionalism. We are also lucky in that we work with a number of outside business partners that are like extended family. They too sprang into action. Together, we all worked together to ensure one goal: serving our clients.

To say that I am proud of my kids, my friends, my team, and my partners would be a big understatement. They delivered. And I am filled with gratitude towards our clients, the vast majority who stayed with us. It has been many years since Bill left this world for the great

vi | KELLY KELLY

beyond. But I know he is with us. During this time, I have made many mistakes, but I know I also have made many good decisions, too.

Over time, I experienced the entire range of emotions one does after losing a loved one. I did do a lot of grieving. I did a lot of soul searching. And at times I had a lot of self-doubt. Yes, my mind occasionally meanders to that space. I believe that's normal. But here's what I tell myself. I am still standing. The firm is still standing. Our clients are still standing.

While this book is dedicated to Bill's memory, it is also dedicated to your future. For those of you new to the whole dizzying world of retirement planning, I hope this first gives you a sense of our values and our mission. And I also hope it gives you a better sense of what we do and how we can help you. I am more committed than ever to continue what we started way back when. Despite all the challenges, setbacks, the successes, I will always remain forever young, hopeful, and thankful.

You too can retire your fear and plan your future.

I am reminded of a story that I had almost forgotten about. Shortly after Bill was buried on Halloween in 2017, a group of close friends, family, and some of my team, gathered back at our house to remember Bill. It was a long and emotionally draining day and it gave all of us a chance to laugh and cry and reflect on the fact that life is short, but it is also a blessing. In particular, I was blessed. I understood, in that moment, that it was now time for me to carry on.

Soon, it was getting dark and getting late. As the adults were mingling, Young William found John Budris. John was a close friend of Bill's and became the co-host of our financial radio show; he was that avuncular figure every family has, and he became a father-like figure to William. He said to John: "Let's go out trick or treating. Dad wouldn't want me to be sad. He would want us to go." And they did.

It was a very good plan.

Potential Risks to Your Ideal Retirement

Ever feel like life gets in the way and prevents you from doing things you should not ignore? I think if we're honest with ourselves, we've all put off obligations we know are important.

In your case, you may be reading this book because it's time to get serious about financial planning and, specifically, devising a way to best prepare for retirement. A retirement income plan should be based on more components than just your investments or your finances. The preparation of that strategy begins with your desires, ambitions, and goals for this fulfilling season of life.

There's no such thing as a silly question. Not when one of the most common questions we hear from folks regarding retirement is, "Am I going to be okay?" Often, it seems, people are reluctant to meet with financial professionals because they worry they might sound uneducated. Yet, it's understandable for you to be a novice when it comes to financial issues and retirement concerns. You've been busy with your lives and your careers. Time spent away from work has meant time spent being around those you love and engaging in the activities you enjoy. Retirement provides the opportunity to do even more of that, while not fretting over work obligations.

Concerns people have about what they may encounter during retirement can be far-reaching and still perfectly legitimate. For a quick snapshot, I want to provide a brief sampling of wide-ranging issues that can come up during discussions about what to potentially brace for in retirement. This book will touch on many of these issues in further detail.

Politics: A presidential election often stirs emotions regarding potential effects on the economy. Investors grow anxious about how a new president can influence market returns. It's Congress, however, that establishes tax laws and passes spending bills. Yet the president can indirectly affect the economy and the stock market in various ways such as the appointment of policymakers, development of international relations, and influential sway on new legislation.

Taxes: An example of a president's influence can be cited in signature legislation passed during Donald Trump's presidency, the Tax Cuts and Jobs Act of 2017. However, our tax system remains progressive, so the more you earn, the higher the tax rate within each tax bracket of subsequently higher income. A thorough understanding of tax regulations can be crucial. A financial professional can help identify potential issues a tax professional can help solve.

Inflation: Government spending, which most recently spiked with relief packages designed to assist U.S. citizens during the COVID-19 pandemic, can fuel concerns of inflationary hikes stemming from an influx of money thrust at the same consumer goods. A retiree's income can be impacted by the effect inflation can have on a fixed budget. The value of currency decreases because inflation erodes purchasing power.

Health pandemic: The coronavirus outbreak could impact how Americans view risks and re-examine healthy habits. That, potentially, could be one of the effects of COVID-19 as we assess how long a pandemic can last and if others will occur in our lifetimes. The cost of health care can be surprising throughout retirement. It could become an issue people focus on even more following the pandemic, which had a particularly acute impact on some U.S. elder care facilities.

Cybersecurity: Think you'll give up your smartphone in retirement? No way, right? It's here to stay, along with other intellectual gadgetry, including devices that have not been patented or invented. Retirees are becoming more tech-savvy, yet they can also be more trusting, which can be problematic when responding to potential scammers by phone, text, or email. Cybercrime often uses technology to target potential victims. Scammers, much like technology, figure to only grow more sophisticated over time.

CHAPTER 1

Longevity

Y ou would think the prospect of the grave would loom more frightening as we age, yet many retirees say their number one concern is actually running out of money in their twilight years.[1] This concern is, unfortunately, justified, in part, because of one significant factor: We're living longer.

According to the Social Security Administration's 2011 Trustee Report, in 1950, the average life expectancy for a sixty-five-year-old man was seventy-eight, and the average for a sixty-five-year-old woman was eighty-one. Those averages were expected to be eighty-three and eighty-six, respectively by the year 2021.[2]

The bottom line of many retirees' budget woes comes down to this: They just didn't plan to live so long. Now, when we are younger and in our working years, that's not something we necessarily see as a bad thing; don't some people fantasize about living forever or, at least, reaching the ripe old age of one hundred?

However, with a longer lifespan, as we near retirement, we face a few snags. Our resources are finite—we only have so much money to provide income—but our lifespans can be unpredictably long, perhaps longer than our resources allow. Also, longer lives don't necessarily equate with healthier lives. The longer you live, the more

---

[1] Liz Weston. nerdwallet.com. March 25, 2021. "Will You Really Run Out of Money in Retirement?" https://www.nerdwallet.com/article/finance/will-you-really-run-out-of-money-in-retirement

[2] Social Security Administration. 2011 Trustees Report. "Actuarial Publications: Cohort Life Expectancy." https://www.ssa.gov/OACT/TR/2011/lr5a4.html

money you will likely need to spend on health care, even excluding long-term care needs like nursing homes.

You also will run into inflation. If you don't plan to live another twenty-five years but end up doing so, inflation at an average 3 percent will approximately double the price of goods over that time period. Put a harsh twist on that, and the buying power of a ninety-year-old will be half of what they possessed if they retired at sixty-five.[3]

Because we don't necessarily get to have our cake and eat it, too, our collective increased longevity hasn't necessarily increased the healthy years of our lives. Typically, our life-extending care most widely applies to the time in our lives where we will need more care in general. Think of common situations like a pacemaker at eighty-five, or cancer treatment at seventy-eight.

"Wow, Kelly," I can hear you say. "Way to start with the good news first."

I know, I've painted a grim picture, but all I'm concerned about here is cost. It's hard to put a dollar sign on life, but that is essentially what we're talking about when discussing longevity and finances. Living longer isn't a bad thing; it just costs more, and one key to a sound retirement strategy is preparing for it in advance.

Let me share a story with you about Michael and Donna and the value of thinking strategically about longevity.

Michael works for an area utility company, and Donna is retired from the banking industry. Both are fortunate to have pensions, and their healthy salary history translates to a better than average level of projected Social Security income. The couple has done a very good job of saving and accumulating—today at ages sixty-nine and seventy they have amassed a little over $1.8 million in their nest egg. They have three traditional IRA accounts, a 457(b) and over a half a million in cash at the bank. The couple also owns some income property that generates about $1,500 per month in positive cash flow.

---

[3] Bob Sullivan, Benjamin Curry. Forbes. April 28, 2021. "Inflation And Retirement Investments: What You Need to Know."
https://www.forbes.com/advisor/retirement/inflation-retirement-investments/

During their first meeting with Kelly Financial, the couple presented us with Social Security Statements, pension documents, and investment statements. They also completed our pre-meeting homework assignment and itemized their monthly household expenses. We entered this information into our planning software in order to answer the following questions: Does the couple run out of money in retirement and if so, when? And what rate of return allows the nest egg to accommodate expenses and provide the lifestyle the couple desires during their golden years?

This analysis provided Michael and Donna with immediate peace of mind. It is our experience that most folks we work with have done some good things over the years. Now, they just want to know what it all means combined with the assurances that they are "okay" or they are on the right track.

Michael and Donna were very pleased to have that objective look at their situation.

In addition, Michael expressed to us that it was important for Donna to feel comfortable with the people managing their money in the event he predeceases her.

The results were very comforting to this couple. They should not run out of money all the way through age 100, and their modest level of household expenses will provide them with a positive monthly surplus, which means pension income, Social Security income, and real estate income will outpace their projected monthly expenses (which we inflated at 2.5 percent per year) by a healthy margin.

So, Michael and Donna are in a somewhat unique position. They don't have to tap into their nest egg in retirement aside from IRS required minimum distributions that kick in at age seventy-three. This means they have the luxury of choice—they can leave the nest egg in cash, leverage guaranteed offerings to simply keep pace with inflation or invest because they can afford to take market risk knowing they have no need to tap into the funds.

Yes, Michael and Donna were blessed with their jobs and the income generated by those jobs. But the moral of this story is that early on they planned for the long term. I don't like cliches but this one sums up their path: they saw the forest before the trees.

Retiring Early

A key part of planning for retirement revolves around retirement income. After all, retirement is cutting the cord that tethers you to your employer—and your monthly check. However, that check often comes with many other benefits, particularly health care. Health care is often the thing that can unexpectedly put dreams for an early retirement on hold. Some employers offer health benefits to their retired workers, but that number has declined drastically over the past several decades. In 1988, among employers who offered health benefits to their workers, 66 percent offered health benefits to their retirees. By 2020, that number had since diminished to 29 percent.[4]

So, with employer-offered retirement health benefits on the wane, this becomes a major point of concern for anyone who is looking to retire, particularly those who are looking to retire before age sixty-five, when they would become eligible for Medicare coverage. Fidelity estimates that the average retired couple at age sixty-five will need approximately $300,000 for health care expenses in retirement, not including long-term care.[5] Do you think it's likely that cost will decrease?

Even if you are working until age sixty-five or have plans to cover your health expenses until that point, I often have clients who incorrectly assume Medicare is their golden ticket to cover all expenses. That is simply not the case.

Retiring Later

Planning for a long life in retirement partly depends on when you retire. While many people end up retiring earlier than they

---

[4] Henry J. Kaiser Family Foundation. October 8, 2020. "2020 Employer Health Benefits Survey Section Eleven: Retiree Health Benefits." https://www.kff.org/report-section/ehbs-2020-section-11-retiree-health-benefits/
[5] Fidelity Viewpoints. Fidelity. May 6, 2021. "How to Plan for Rising Health Care Costs." https://www.fidelity.com/viewpoints/personal-finance/plan-for-rising-health-care-costs

anticipated—due to injuries, layoffs, family crises, and other unforeseen circumstances—continuing to work past age sixty (and even sixty-five) is still a viable option for others and can be an excellent way to help establish financial comfort in retirement.

There are many reasons for this. For one, you obviously still earn a paycheck and the benefits accompanying it. Medical coverage and beefing up your retirement accounts with further savings can be significant by themselves but continuing your income also should keep you from dipping into your retirement funds, further allowing them the opportunity to grow.

Additionally, for many workers, their nine-to-five job is more than just clocking in and out. Having a sense of purpose can keep us active physically, mentally, and socially. That kind of activity and level of engagement may also help stave off many of the health problems that plague retirees. Avoiding a sedentary life is one of the advantages of staying plugged into the workforce, if possible.

The pandemic has, at least temporarily, thrown chaos into the retirement sphere on so many levels. One of the starker examples is the senior worker. Over the last year, I have learned about a new phenomenon called "unretire" and the birth of the "encore entrepreneur."

According to a 2021 Pew Research Center study: "The leading edge of the Baby Boomer generation reached age sixty-two (the age at which workers can claim Social Security) in 2008. Between 2008 and 2019, the retired population ages fifty-five and older grew by about 1 million retirees per year. In the past two years, the ranks of retirees fifty-five and older have grown by 3.5 million."[6]

This development seemed to defy prior predictions.

In May 2017, the Bureau of Labor Statistics in fact estimated that the labor participation rate "is expected to increase fastest for the oldest segments of the population—most notably, people ages sixty-

---

[6] Richard Fry. Pew Research Center. November 4, 2021. "Amid the pandemic, a rising share of older U.S. adults are now retired." https://www.pewresearch.org/fact-tank/2021/11/04/amid-the-pandemic-a-rising-share-of-older-u-s-adults-are-now-retired/

five to seventy-four and seventy-five and older—through 2024."[7] For nearly a quarter-century before COVID-19 struck, the trend was for older workers to remain in the labor force.

There were a number of reasons why people remained in the labor force longer. But perhaps the most influential was the following: Decline in wealth effect—especially after The Great Recession (2008-2009).

Remember that in 2000, the dot.com bubble burst, and many people's retirement savings were impacted. And fewer than ten years later, America experienced a disastrous recession. For older workers, the ten-year period from 2000 up to and including 2009 was particularly hard on their savings, and their home values plummeted, too. The first baby boomers were to turn sixty-five in early 2011. The net result of this was that older workers remained in the labor force longer to make up lost savings and wait for home values to regain their pre-recession levels.

But COVID-19 changed things. Older workers were dropping out of the labor force at a much faster pace than they had been prior to the pandemic. Again, there are a number of factors to explain this fact. Understandably, older people were more susceptible to getting the virus, so they stayed out of work. But perhaps the biggest factor is that they could afford to drop out of the labor force. Unlike 2008-2009, home prices continued their frenzied climb during the pandemic. And aside from a brief plunge in the market during the earliest part of the pandemic, the market rose to record highs through the end of 2021. In short, people largely did not see a diminution of their wealth. The economy may have crashed, but their retirement assets did not. They were able stop working.

The real question to ask is, will this be part of a longer-term trend, or will older workers return to the workplace, also known as unretiring?

---

[7] Mitra Toossi and Elka Torpey. U.S. Bureau of Labor Statistics. May 2017. "Older workers: Labor force trends and career options." https://www.bls.gov/careeroutlook/2017/article/older-workers.htm

Older workers may in fact be returning to the workplace. For one, there has been a lot of wealth destruction with the markets in 2022. Many may be forced to return to work. On the other hand, something else might be at play.

In June 2021, prnewswire.com reported that people age fifty-five-plus make up 21 percent of the U.S. population "but own a disproportionately high 50.9 percent of U.S. small businesses."[8] Enter the encore entrepreneur.

And while there are funding opportunities and business financing vehicles to start these small businesses, many older workers prefer to rely on personal finances, including savings (74 percent of encore entrepreneurs) and credit cards (36.6 percent of encore entrepreneurs). Tellingly, these workers "are also 52.3 percent more likely to finance their business using retirement savings, compared to younger groups," writes PR Newswire.

Here is another rather fascinating datapoint. The number of small business applications just hit a record in 2021. Conceivably, then, there may be a significant number of older workers who either leave their jobs to start their own business or who unretire to start their own business.

These developments are enthralling. And they can certainly play a role in determining whether one retires early, retires later, or, as we now know, simply unretires.

Health Care

Take a second to reflect on your health care plan. Although working up to or even past age sixty-five would allow you to avoid a coverage gap between your working years and Medicare, that may not be an option for you. Even if it is, when you retire, you will need to make some decisions about what kind of insurance coverage you may need

---

[8] PR Newswire. June 3, 2021. "Older Entrepreneurs Own Half of U.S. Small Businesses, Bootstrap With Personal Savings, Credit Cards and Retirement Funds." https://www.prnewswire.com/news-releases/older-entrepreneurs-own-half-of-us-small-businesses-bootstrap-with-personal-savings-credit-cards-and-retirement-funds-301305324.html

to supplement your Medicare. Are there any medical needs you have that may require coverage in addition to Medicare? Did your parents or grandparents have any inherited medical conditions you might consider using a special savings plan to cover?

These are all questions that are important to review with your financial professional so you can be sure you have enough money put aside for health care.

Long-Term Care

Longevity means the need for long-term care is statistically more likely to happen. If you intend to pass on a legacy, planning for long-term care is paramount, since most estimates project nearly 70 percent of Americans will need some type of it.[9] However, this may be one of the biggest, most stressful pieces of longevity planning I encounter in my work. For one thing, who wants to talk about the point in their lives when they may feel the most limited? Who wants to dwell on what will happen if they no longer can toilet, bathe, dress, or feed themselves?

I get it; this is a less-than-fun part of planning. But a little bit of preparation now can go a long way!

When it comes to your longevity, just like with your goals, one of the important things to do is sit and dream. It may not be the fun, road-trip-to-the-Grand-Canyon kind of dreaming, but you can spend time envisioning how you want your twilight years to look.

For instance, if it is important for you to live in your home for as long as possible, who will provide for the day-to-day fixes and to-dos of housework if you become ill? Will you set aside money for a service, or do you have relatives or friends nearby whom you could comfortably allow to help you? Do you prefer in-home care over a nursing home or assisted living? This could be a good time to discuss the possibility of moving into a retirement community versus staying

---

[9] LongTermCare.gov. February 18, 2020. "How Much Care Will You Need?" https://acl.gov/ltc/basic-needs/how-much-care-will-you-need

where you are or whether it's worth moving to another state and leaving relatives behind.

These are all important factors to discuss with your spouse and children, as *now* is the right time to address questions and concerns. For instance, is aging in place more important to one spouse than the other? Are the friends or relatives who live nearby emotionally, physically, and financially capable of helping you for a time if you face an illness?

Many families I meet with find these conversations very uncomfortable, particularly when children discuss nursing home care with their parents. A knee-jerk reaction for many is to promise they will care for their aging parents. This is noble and well-intentioned, but there needs to be an element of realism here. Does "help" from an adult child mean they stop by and help you with laundry, cooking, home maintenance, and bills? Or does it mean they move you into their spare room when you have hip surgery? Are they prepared to help you use the restroom and bathe if that becomes difficult for you to do on your own?

I don't mean to discourage families from caring for their own; this can be a profoundly admirable relationship when it works out. However, I've seen families put off planning for late-in-life care based on a tenuous promise that the adult children would care for their parents, only to watch as the support system crumbles. Sometimes this is because the assumed caregiver hasn't given serious thought to the preparation they would need, both in a formal sense and regarding their personal physical, emotional, and financial commitments. This is often also because we can't see the future: Alzheimer's disease and other maladies of old age can exact a heavy toll. When a loved one reaches the point where he or she is at risk of wandering away or needs help with two or more activities of daily living, it can be more than one person or family can realistically handle.

If you know what you want, communicate with your family about both the best-case and worst-case scenarios. Then, hope for the best, and plan for the worst.

Realistic Cost of Care

Wrapped up in your planning should be a consideration for the cost of long-term care. One study estimates that by 2030, the nation's long-term care costs could reach $2.5 trillion as roughly 24 million Americans require some type of long-term care.[10] The potential costs for such care and treatment can be underestimated, especially by those who have maintained robust health and find it difficult to envision future declines to their condition.

Another piece of planning for long-term care costs is anticipating inflation. It's common knowledge that prices have been and keep rising, which can lower your purchasing power on everything from food to medical care. Long-term care is a big piece of the inflation-disparity pie.

While local costs vary from state to state, here's the national median for various forms of long-term care (plus projections that account for a 3 percent annual inflation, so you can see what I am referencing):[11]

---

[10] Tara O'Neill Hayes, Sara Kurtovic. Americanactionforum.org. February 18, 2020. "The Ballooning Costs of Long-Term Care." https://www.americanactionforum.org/research/the-ballooning-costs-of-long-term-care/

[11] Genworth Financial. January 2022. "Cost of Care Survey 2021." https://www.genworth.com/aging-and-you/finances/cost-of-care.html

Long-Term Care Costs: Inflation				
	Home Health Care, Homemaker Services	Adult Day Care	Assisted Living	Nursing Home (semi-private room)
Annual 2021	$59,488	$20,280	$54,000	$94,900
Annual 2031	$79,947	$27,255	$72,571	$127,538
Annual 2041	$107,442	$36,628	$97,530	$171,400
Annual 2051	$144,393	$49,225	$131,072	$230,347

Fund Your Long-Term Care

One critical mistake I see are those who haven't planned for long-term care because they assume the government will provide everything. But that's a big misconception. The government has two health insurance programs: Medicare and Medicaid. These can greatly assist you in your health care needs in retirement but usually don't provide enough coverage to cover all your health care costs in retirement. My firm isn't a government outpost, so we don't get to make decisions when it comes to forming policy and specifics about either one of these programs. I'm going to give an overview of both, but if you want to dive into the details of these programs, you can visit www.Medicare.gov and www.Medicaid.gov.

Medicare

Medicare covers those aged sixty-five and older and those who are disabled. Medicare's coverage of any nursing-home-related health issues is limited. It might cover your nursing home stay if it is not a "custodial" stay, and it isn't long-term. For example, if you break a bone or suffer a stroke, stay in a nursing home for rehabilitative care, and then return home, Medicare may cover you. But, if you have developed dementia or are looking to move to a nursing facility because you can no longer bathe, dress, toilet, feed yourself, or take care of your hygiene, etc., then Medicare is not going to pay for your nursing home costs.[12]

You can enroll in Medicare anytime during the three months before and three months after your sixty-fifth birthday. Miss your enrollment deadline, and you could risk paying increased premiums for the rest of your life.[13] On top of prompt enrollment, there are a few other things to think about when it comes to Medicare, not least among them being the need to understand the different "parts," what they do, and what they don't cover.

Part A

Medicare Part A is what you might think of as "classic" Medicare. Hospital care, some types of home health care, and major medical care fall under this. While most enrollees pay nothing for this service (as they likely paid into the system for at least ten years), you may end up paying, either based on work history or delayed signup. In 2022, the highest premium is $499 per month, and a hospital stay does have a deductible, $1,556.[14] And, if you have a hospital stay that surpasses sixty days, you could be looking at additional costs; keep in mind, Medicare doesn't pay for long-term care and services.

---

[12] Medicare.gov. "What Part A covers." https://www.medicare.gov/what-medicare-covers/part-a/what-part-a-covers.html

[13] Medicare.gov. "When can I sign up for Medicare?" https://www.medicare.gov/basics/get-started-with-medicare/sign-up/when-can-i-sign-up-for-medicare

[14] Medicare. "Medicare 2022 Costs at a Glance." https://www.medicare.gov/your-medicare-costs/medicare-costs-at-a-glance

Part B

Medicare Part B is an essential piece of wrap-around coverage for Medicare Part A. It helps pay for doctor visits and outpatient services. This also comes with a price tag: Although the Part B deductible is only $233 in 2022, you will still pay 20 percent of all costs after that, with no limit on out-of-pocket expenses.[15]

Part C

Medicare Part C, more commonly known as Medicare Advantage plans, are an alternative to a combination of Parts A, B, and sometimes D. Administered through private insurance companies, these have a variety of costs and restrictions, and they are subject to the specific policies and rules of the issuing carrier.

Part D

Medicare Part D is also through a private insurer and is supplemental to Parts A and B, as its primary purpose is to cover prescription drugs. Like any private insurance plan, Part D has its quirks and rules that vary from insurer to insurer.

The Donut Hole

Even with a "Part D" in place, you may still have a coverage gap between what your Part D private drug insurance pays for your prescription and what basic Medicare pays. In 2022, the coverage gap is $4,430, meaning, after you meet your private prescription insurance limit, you will spend no more than 25 percent of your drug costs out-of-pocket before Medicare will kick in to pay for more prescription drugs.[16]

---

[15] Ibid.

[16] Medicare. "Costs in the coverage gap."
https://www.medicare.gov/drug-coverage-part-d/costs-for-medicare-drug-coverage/costs-in-the-coverage-gap

Medicare Supplements

Medicare Supplement Insurance, MedSupp, Medigap, or plans labeled Medicare Part F, G, H, I, J . . . Known by a variety of monikers, this is just a fancy way of saying "medical coverage for those over sixty-five that picks up the tab for whatever the federal Medicare program(s) doesn't." Again, costs, limitations, etc., vary by carrier.

Does that sound like a bunch of government alphabet soup to you? It certainly does to me. And did you read the fine print? Unpredictable costs, varied restrictions, difficult-to-compare benefits, donut holes, and coverage gaps. That's par for the course with health care plans through the course of our adult lives. What gives? I thought Medicare was supposed to be easier, comprehensive, and at no cost!

The truth is there is no stage of life when health care is easy to understand.

The best thing you can do for yourself is to scope out the health care field early, compare costs often, and prepare for out-of-pocket costs well in advance—decades, if possible.

Medicaid

Medicaid is a program the states administer, so funding, protocol, and limitations vary. Compared to Medicare, Medicaid more widely covers nursing home care, but it targets a different demographic: those with low incomes.

If you have more assets than the Medicaid limit in your state and need nursing home care, you will need to use those assets to pay for your care. You also will have a list of additional state-approved ways to spend some of these assets over the Medicaid limit, such as pre-purchasing burial plots and funeral expenses or paying off debts. After that, your remaining assets fund your nursing home stay until they are gone, at which point Medicaid will jump in.

Some people aren't stymied by this, thinking they will just pass on their financial assets early, gifting them to relatives, friends, and causes so they can qualify for Medicaid when they need it. However, to prevent this exact scenario, Uncle Sam has implemented the look-back period. Currently, if you enroll in Medicaid, you are subject to having the government scrutinize the last five years of your finances for large gifts or expenses that may subject you to penalties, temporarily making you ineligible for Medicaid coverage.

So, if you're planning to preserve your money for future generations and retain control of your financial resources during your lifetime, you'll probably want to prepare for the costs of longevity beyond a "government plan."

Self-Funding

One way to fund a longer life is the old-fashioned way, through self-funding. There are a variety of financial tools you can use, and they all have their pros and cons. If your assets are in low-interest financial vehicles (savings, bonds, CDs), you risk letting inflation erode the value of your dollar. Or, if you are relying on the stock market, you have more growth potential, but you'll also want to consider the possible implications of market volatility. What if your assets take a hit? If you suffer a loss in your retirement portfolio in early or mid-retirement, you might have the option to "tighten your belt," so to speak, and cut back on discretionary spending to allow your portfolio the room to bounce back. But, if you are retired and depend on income from a stock account that just hit a downward stride, what are you going to do?

HSAs

These days, you might also be able to self-fund through a health savings account, or HSA, if you have access to one through a high-deductible health plan (you will not qualify to save in an HSA after enrolling in Medicare). In an HSA, any growth of your tax-deductible contributions will be tax-free, and any distributions paid out for qualified health costs are also tax-free. Long-term care expenses count as health costs, so, if this is an option available to you, it is one way to use the tax advantages to self-fund your longevity. Bear in mind, if you are younger than sixty-five, any money you use for nonqualified expenses will be subject to taxes and penalties, and, if you are older than sixty-five, any HSA money you use for non-medical expenses is subject to income tax.

LTCI

One slightly more nuanced way to pay for longevity, specifically for long-term care, is long-term care insurance, or LTCI. As car insurance protects your assets in case of a car accident and home insurance protects your assets in case something happens to your house, long-term care insurance aims to protect your assets in case you need long-term care in an at-home or nursing home situation.

As with other types of insurance, you will pay a monthly or annual premium in exchange for an insurance company paying for long-term care down the road. Typically, policies cover two to three years of care, which is adequate for an "average" situation: it's estimated 70 percent of Americans will need about three years of long-term care of some kind. However, it's important to consider you might not be "average" when you are preparing for long-term care costs; on average, 20 percent of today's sixty-five-year-olds could need care for longer than five years.[17]

Now, there are a few oft-cited components of LTCI that make it unattractive for some:

- Expense — LTCI can be expensive. It is generally less expensive the younger you are, but a fifty-five-year-old couple who purchased LTCI in 2022 could expect to pay $2,080 each year for an average three-year coverage policy. And the annual cost only increases from there the older you are.[18]

- Limited options — Let's face it: LTCI may be expensive for consumers, but it can also be expensive for companies that

---

[17] LongTermCare.gov. February 18, 2020. "How Much Care Will You Need?" https://acl.gov/ltc/basic-needs/how-much-care-will-you-need

[18] American Association for Long-Term Care Insurance. 2022. "Long-Term Care Insurance Facts-Data-Statistics-2022 Reports." https://www.aaltci.org/long-term-care-insurance/learning-center/ltcfacts-2022.php#2022costs

offer it. With fewer companies willing to take on that expense, this narrows the market, meaning opportunities to price shop for policies with different options or custom benefits are limited.

- If you know you need it, you might not be able to get it — Insurance companies offering LTCI are taking on a risk that you may need it. That risk is the foundation of the product—you may or may not need LTCI. If you know you will need it because you have a dementia diagnosis or another illness for which you will need long-term care, you likely won't qualify for LTCI.

- Use it or lose it — If you have LTCI and are in the minority of Americans who die having never needed long-term care, all the money you paid into your LTCI policy is gone.

- Possibly fluctuating rates — Your rate is not locked in on LTCI. Companies maintain the ability to raise or lower your premium amounts. This means some seniors face an ultimatum: Keep funding a policy at what might be a less affordable rate *or* lose coverage and let go of all the money they paid in so far.

After that, you might be thinking, "How can people possibly be interested in LTCI?" But let me repeat myself—as many as 70 percent of Americans will need long-term care. And, although only one in ten Americans have purchased LTCI, keep in mind the high cost of nursing home care. Can you afford $7,000 a month to put into nursing home care and still have enough left over to protect your legacy? This is a very real concern considering one set of statistics reported a two-in-three chance that a senior citizen will become physically or cognitively impaired in their lifetime.[19] So, not to sound like a broken record, but it is vitally important to have a plan in place to deal with longevity and long-term care if you intend to leave a financial legacy.

---

[19] payingforseniorcare.com. 2022. "Long-Term Senior Care Statistics." https://www.payingforseniorcare.com/statistics

A few relevant statistics to keep in mind:

- The longer you live, the more likely you are to continue living; the longer you live, the more health care you will likely need to pay for.
- The average cost of a private nursing home room in the United States in 2021 was $9,034 a month.[20] But keep in mind, that is just the nursing home—it doesn't include other medical costs, let alone pleasantries, like entertainment or hobby spending.
- In 2021, Fidelity calculated that a healthy couple retiring at age sixty-five could expect to pay around $300,000 over the course of retirement to cover health and medical expenses.
- The average man will need $143,00, and the average woman needs about 10 percent more, or $157,000, because of women's longer life expectancies.[21]

I know. Whoa, there, Kelly, I was hoping to have a realistic idea of health costs, not be driven over by a cement mixer!

The good news is, while we don't know these exact costs in advance, we know there *will* be costs. And you won't have to pay your total Medicare lifetime premiums in one day as a lump sum. Now that you have a good idea of health care costs in retirement, you can *plan* for them! That's the real point, here: Planning in advance can keep you from feeling nickel-and-dimed to your wits' end. Instead, having a sizeable portion of your assets earmarked for health care can allow you the freedom to choose health care networks, coverage options, and long-term care possibilities you like and that you think offer you the best in life.

---

[20] Genworth Financial. January 31, 2022. "Genworth 2020 Cost of Care Survey." https://www.genworth.com/aging-and-you/finances/cost-of-care.html

[21] Elizabeth O'Brien. Money. May 10, 2021. "Health Care Now Costs Couples $300,000 in Retirement, According to Fidelity's Latest Estimate." https://money.com/health-care-costs-retirement-fidelity-2021-study/. The $300,000 estimate assumes an opposite-gender couple, where the man lives until age 87 and the woman until age 89.

Product Riders

LTCI and self-funding are not the only ways to plan for the expenses of longevity. Some companies are getting creative with their products, particularly insurance companies. One way they are retooling to meet people's needs is through optional product riders on annuities and life insurance. Elsewhere in this book, I talk about annuity basics, but here's a brief overview: Annuities are insurance contracts. You pay the insurance company a premium, either as a lump sum or as a series of payments over a set amount of time, in exchange for guaranteed income payments. One of the advantages of an annuity is it has access to riders, which allow you to tweak your contract for a fee, usually about 1 percent of the contract value annually. One annuity rider some companies offer is a long-term care rider. If you have an annuity with a long-term care rider and are not in need of long-term care, your contract behaves as any annuity contract would—nothing changes. Generally speaking, if you reach a point when you can't perform multiple functions of daily life on your own, you notify the insurance company, and a representative will turn on those provisions of your contract.

Like LTCI, different companies and products offer different options. Some annuity long-term care riders offer coverage of two years in a nursing home situation. Others cap expenses at two times the original annuity's value. It greatly depends. Some people prefer this option because there isn't a "use-it-or-lose-it" piece; if you die without ever having needed long-term care, you still will have had the income benefit from the base contract. Still, as with any annuities or insurance contracts, there are the usual restrictions and limitations. Withdrawing money from the contract will affect future income payments, early distributions can result in a penalty, income taxes may apply, and, because the insurance company's solvency is what guarantees your payments, it's important to do your research about the insurance company you are considering purchasing a contract from.

Understandably, a discussion on long-term care is bound to feel at least a little tedious. Yet, this is a critical piece of planning for income in retirement, particularly if you want to leave a legacy.

Spousal Planning

Here's one thing to keep in mind no matter how you plan to save: Many of us will be planning for more than ourselves. Look back at all the stats on health events and the likelihood of long life and long-term care. If they hold true for a single individual, then the likelihood of having a costly health or long-term care event is even higher for a married couple. You'll be planning for not just one life, but two. So, when it comes to long-term care insurance, annuities, self-funding, or whatever strategy you are looking at using, be sure you are funding longevity for the both of you.

CHAPTER 2

Taxes

Where to begin with taxes? Perhaps by acknowledging we all bear responsibility for the resources we share. Roads, bridges, schools... It is the patriotic duty of every American to pay their fair share of taxes. Many would agree with me. However, while they don't mind paying their fair share, they're not interested in paying one cent more than that!

Now, just talking taxes probably takes your mind to April—tax season. You are probably thinking about all the forms you collect and how you file. Perhaps you are thinking about your certified public accountant or another qualified tax professional and saying to yourself, "I've already got taxes taken care of, thanks!"

However, what I see when people come into my office is that their relationship with their tax professional is purely a January through April relationship. That means they may have a tax professional, but not a tax *planner*.

What I mean is tax planning extends beyond filing taxes. In April, we are required to settle our accounts with the IRS to make sure we have paid up on our bill or to even the score if we have overpaid. But real tax planning is about making each financial move in a way that allows you to keep the most money in your pocket and out of Uncle Sam's.

Now, as a caveat, I want to emphasize I am neither a CPA nor a tax planner; the advisors at Kelly Financial are not tax professionals, either. But I see the way taxes affect my clients, and we have plenty of experience helping clients implement tax-efficient strategies in their retirement plans in conjunction with their tax professionals.

We maintain relationships with tax professionals for the benefit of our clients who may need their expertise and assistance. In addition, our experience has taught us that many of our clients have established relationships with tax professionals. In both instances, we recognize the significance of having open communications among client, tax professional, and financial advisor to help ensure that the clients are well served. It is good to remember that Kelly Financial is a fiduciary, so our clients' interests come before our own.

It is especially important to me to help my clients develop tax-efficient strategies in their retirement plans because each dollar they can keep in their pockets is a dollar we can put to work.

Two strategies come to mind: Withdrawal sequence ordering, and tax bracket management

Withdrawal sequence ordering is the strategy that determines when a particular investment account should be used for income. The basic guidelines around withdrawal order are as follows: taxable accounts first; tax-deferred accounts, next; and then, tax-exempt accounts.

The objective of tax bracket management is to try to fill up lower tax brackets with taxable income and then potentially take from areas with better tax treatment to fill any spending gaps without moving unnecessarily into a higher tax bracket.

Again, to reiterate, our financial advisors are not tax experts or CPAs, but they have a solid understanding of the tax code. Knowing this, they apply the tax code when designing retirement plans. And to emphasize this point: we always recommend clients consult with a tax professional to get their opinion as the financial advisors implement different retirement planning strategies.

The Fed

Now, in the United States, taxes can be a rather uncertain proposition. Depending on who is in the White House and which party controls Congress, we might be tempted to assume tax rates could either decline or increase in the next four to eight years accordingly. However, there is one (large!) factor we, as a nation, must confront: the national debt.

Currently, according to USDebtClock.org, we are over $29,000,000,000,000 in debt and climbing. That's $29 *trillion* with a "T." With just $1 trillion, you could park it in the bank at a zero percent interest rate and spend more than $54 million every day for fifty years without hitting a zero balance.

Even if Congress got a handle and stopped that debt from its daily compound, divided by each taxpayer, we each would owe about $214,000. So, will that be check, cash, or Venmo?

My point here isn't to give you anxiety. I'm just cautioning you that even with the rosiest of outlooks on our personal income tax rates, none of us should count on low tax rates for the long term. Instead, you and your network of professionals (tax, legal, and financial) should constantly be looking for ways to take advantage of tax-saving opportunities as they come. After all, the best "luck" is when proper planning meets opportunity.

So, how can we get started?

Know Your Limits

One of the foundational pieces of tax planning is knowing what tax bracket you are in, based on your income after subtracting pre-tax or untaxed assets. Your income taxes are based on your taxable income.

One reason to know your taxable income and your income tax rate is so you can see how far away you are from the next lower or higher tax bracket. This is particularly important when it comes to decisions such as gifting and Roth IRA rollovers.

For instance, based on the 2022 tax table, Mallory and Ralph's taxable income is just over $345,000, putting them in the 32 percent tax bracket and about $4,900 above the upper end of the 24 percent tax bracket. They have already maxed out their retirement funds' tax-exempt contributions for the year. Their daughter, Gloria, is a sophomore in college. This couple could shave a considerable amount off their tax bill if they use the $4,900 to help Gloria out with groceries and school—something they were likely to do, anyway, but now can deliberately be put to work for them in their overall financial strategy.

Now, I use Mallory and Ralph only as an example—your circumstances are probably different—but I think this nicely illustrates the way planning ahead for taxes can save you money.

Assuming a Lower Tax Rate

Many people anticipate being in a lower tax bracket in retirement. It makes sense: You won't be contributing to retirement funds; you'll be drawing from them. And you won't have all those work expenses—work clothes, transportation, lunch meetings, etc.

Yet do you really plan on changing your lifestyle after retirement? Do you plan to cut down on the number of times you eat out, scale back vacations, and skimp on travel?

What I see in my office is many couples spend more in the first few years, or maybe the first decade, of retirement. Sure, that may taper off later on, but usually only just in time for their budget to be hit with greater health and long-term care expenses. Do you see where this is going? Many people plan as though their taxable income will be lower in retirement and are surprised when the tax bills come in and look more or less the same as they used to. It's better to plan for the worst and hope for the best, wouldn't you agree?

401(k)/IRA

One sometimes-unexpected piece of tax planning in retirement concerns your 401(k) or IRA. Most of us have one of these accounts or an equivalent. Throughout our working lives, we pay in, dutifully socking away a portion of our earnings in these tax-deferred accounts. There's the rub: tax deferred. Not tax-free. Very rarely is anything free of taxation when you get down to it. Using 401(k)s and IRAs in retirement is no different. The taxes the government deferred when you were in your working years are now coming due, and you will pay taxes on that income at whatever your current tax rate is.

Just to ensure Uncle Sam gets his due, the government also has a required minimum distribution, or RMD, rule. Beginning at age seventy-three, you are required to withdraw a certain minimum amount every year from your 401(k) or IRA, or else you will face a 50 percent tax penalty on any RMD monies you should have withdrawn but didn't—and that's on top of income tax.

Of course, there is also the Roth account. The Roth IRA is named after the late Delaware Sen. William Roth. It became a savings option in 1998. Roth accounts were conceived as a way to increase access to tax-advantaged retirement accounts without substantially reducing government revenue in the short term.

One phrase you might have come across is the "Roth Conversion."

Between clients and prospective clients who inquire about Roths, questions about converting from a traditional IRA to a Roth IRA are among the most often asked of our advisors. Unfortunately, it is not a quick "yes" or "no" answer. The strategy of employing a Roth involves a good amount of analysis.

With a Roth, you contribute after-tax dollars and get tax-free withdrawals in retirement. Creating a tax-free stream of income is a powerful retirement tool. These types of accounts offer big benefits, but the rules for Roths can be complex. Speaking with a financial professional about the pros and cons of a Roth account is a good first step before you consider this option.

You can think of the difference between a Roth and a traditional retirement account as the difference between taxing the seed and taxing the harvest. Because Roths are funded with post-tax dollars, there aren't tax penalties for early withdrawals of the principal nor are there taxes on the growth after you reach age fifty-nine-and-one-half. Perhaps best of all, there are no RMDs. Of course, you must own a Roth account for a minimum of five years before you are able to take advantage of all its features.

This is one more area where it pays to be aware of your tax bracket. Some people may find it advantageous to "convert" their traditional retirement account funds to Roth account funds in a year during that they are in a lower tax bracket. Others may opt to put any excess RMDs from their traditional retirement accounts into other products, like stocks or insurance.

Does that make your head spin? Understandable. That's why it's so important to work with a financial professional and tax planner who can help you execute these sorts of tax-efficient strategies and help you understand what you are doing and why.

CHAPTER 3

Market Volatility

U p and down. Roller coaster. Merry-go-round. Bulls and
bears. Peak-to-trough.

Sound familiar? This is the language we use to talk about
the stock market. With volatility and spikes, even our language is
jarring, bracing, and vivid.

Still, financial strategies tend to revolve around market-based
products, for good reasons. For one thing, there is no other financial
class that packs the same potential for growth, pound for pound, as
stock-based products. Because of growth potential, inflation
protection, and new opportunities, it may be unwise to avoid the
market entirely.

However, along with the potential for growth is the potential for
loss. Many of the people I see in my office come in still feeling a bit
burned from the market drama of 2000 to 2010. That was a rough
stretch, and many of us are once-bitten-twice-shy investors, right?

So how do we balance these factors? How do we try to satisfy both
the need for protection and the need for growth?

For one thing, it is important to recognize the value of diversity.
Now, I'm not just talking about the diversity of assets among
different kinds of stocks, or even different kinds of stocks and bonds.
That's only one kind of diversity; while important, both stocks and
bonds, though different, are both still market-based products. Most
market-based products, even within a diverse portfolio, tend to rise
or lower as a whole, just like an incoming tide. Therefore, a portfolio

diverse in only market-sourced products won't automatically protect your assets during times when the market declines.

In addition to the sort of "horizontal diversity" you have by purchasing a variety of stocks and bonds from different companies, I also suggest you think about "vertical diversity," or diversity among asset classes. This means having different product types, including securities products, bank products, and insurance products—with varying levels of growth potential, liquidity, and protection—all in accordance with your unique situation, goals, and needs.

Market volatility amplifies and accelerates risk.

You might have heard about the "VIX." This volatility index is a measure of market volatility. The Chicago Board Options Exchange (CBOE) is the originator of the CBOE Volatility Index, listed under the ticker symbol (VIX). Sometimes it is referred by its unofficial nickname – the fear index.

The initial VIX was released by CBOE Global Markets in 1993 and is based on a formula that was developed by Vanderbilt University Professor Robert Whaley in 1993.

The VIX is a real-time index to show the expected level of price fluctuation in the S&P 500 Index options over the next 12 months. Times of greater uncertainty (more expected future volatility) result in higher VIX values, while less anxious times correspond with lower values.

While helpful in highlighting market sentiment, the index has its limitations. For instance, it just measures the S&P. It does not measure or reflect expectations in other sectors of the broader market. Arguably, in 2022, the bond market has experienced just as much, if not more, volatility than the S&P Index.

One of the first things we do for people we meet with is provide a free portfolio risk analysis. Using state of the art software tools, we capture your risk tolerance and see if your portfolio fits you. This also involves reviewing goals and objectives and seeing if there is a harmony with your risk tolerance and the composition of your portfolio.

The results of these kinds of exercises can be revealing. We have determined, in some instances, that a client's portfolio contains an unreasonable amount of risk as dictated by their risk tolerance and their long-term goals. And in other instances, conversely, we have determined that certain goals will not be able to be reached precisely because the composition of the portfolio does not allow for the kind of growth needed to attain those goals. Put another way, there was too little risk in the portfolio. (Keep in mind the risk/reward trade-off.)

The Color of Money

When you're looking at the overall diversity of your portfolio, part of the equation is knowing which products fit in what category: what has liquidity, what has protection, and what has growth potential.

Before we dive in, keep in mind these aren't absolutes. You might think of liquidity, growth, and protection as primary colors. While some products will look pretty much yellow, red, or blue, others will have a mix of characteristics, making them more green, orange, or purple.

Growth

I like to think of the growth category as red. It's powerful, it's somewhat volatile, and it's also the category where we have the greatest opportunities for growth and loss. Often, products in the growth category will have a good deal of liquidity but very little protection. These are our market-based products and strategies, and we think of them mostly in shades of red and orange, to designate their growth and liquidity. This is a good place to be when you're young—think fast cars and flashy leather jackets—but its allure often wanes as you move closer to retirement. Examples of "red" products include:

- Stocks
- Equities
- Exchange-traded funds
- Mutual funds

- Corporate bonds
- Real estate investment trusts
- Speculations
- Alternative investments

Liquidity

Yellow is my liquid category color. I typically recommend having at least enough yellow money to cover six months' to a year's worth of expenses in case of emergency. Yellow assets don't need a lot of growth potential; they just need to be readily available when we need them. The "yellow" category includes assets like:

- Cash
- Money market accounts

Protection

The color of protection, to me, is blue. Tranquil, peaceful, sure, even if it lacks a certain amount of flash. This is the direction I like to see people generally move toward as they're nearing retirement. The red, flashy look of stock market returns and the risk of possible overnight losses is less attractive as we near retirement and look for more consistency and reliability. While this category doesn't come with a lot of liquidity, the products here are backed by an insurance company, a bank, or a government entity. "Blue" products include things such as:

- Certificates of deposit (backed by banks)
- Government-based bonds (backed by the U.S. government)
- Life insurance (backed by insurance companies)
- Annuities (backed by insurance companies)

401(k)s

I want to take a second to specifically address a product many retirees will be using to build their retirement income: the 401(k), as well as other retirement accounts. Any of these retirement accounts (IRAs, 401(k)s, 403(b)s, etc.) are basically "tax wrappers." What do I mean by that? Well, depending on your plan provider, a 401(k) could include target-date funds, passively managed products, stocks, bonds, mutual funds, or even variable, fixed, and fixed index annuities, all collected in one place and governed by rules (a.k.a. the "tax wrapper"). These rules govern how much money you can put inside, what ways you can put it in, when you will pay taxes on it, and when you can take the money out. Inside the 401(k), each of the products inside the "tax wrapper" might have its own fees or commissions, in addition to the management fee you pay on the 401(k) itself.

Now, fees can be troublesome. You can't get something for nothing, and fees are how many financial companies and professionals make a living. Yet, it's important to recognize even a fee with a fraction of a percentage point is money out of your pocket—money that represents not just the one-time fee of today but also represents an opportunity cost. A $100,000 IRA that earns 6 percent over a twenty-five-year period without investment fees would earn $430,000. But if just a 0.5 percent fee got factored into that investment, the IRA would be worth $379,000 in twenty-five years, a $50,500 decrease.[22] For someone close to retirement, how much do you think fees may have cost over their lifetime?

Even for those close to retirement, it's important to look at management fees and assess if you think you're getting what you pay for. Over the course of ten years, those costs can add up, and you may have decades ahead of you in which you will need to rely on your assets.

---

[22] Pam Krueger. Kiplinger.com. January 8, 2021. "How to Spot (and Squash) Nasty Fees That Hide in Your Investments."
https://www.kiplinger.com/retirement/retirement-planning/602043/how-to-spot-and-squash-nasty-fees-that-hide-in-your

Dollar-Cost Averaging

With 401(k)s and other market-based retirement products, dollar-cost averaging is a concept that can work in your favor when you are investing for the long term. When the market is trending up, if you are consistently paying in money, month over month, great; your investments can grow, and you are adding to your assets. When the market takes a dip, no problem; your dollars buy more shares at a lower price. At some point, we hope the market will rebound, in which case your shares can grow and possibly be more valuable than they were before. This concept is what we call "dollar-cost averaging." While it can't ensure a profit or guarantee against losses, it's a time-tested strategy for investing in a volatile market.

However, when you are in retirement, this strategy may work against you. You may have heard of "reverse" dollar-cost averaging. Before, when the market lost ground, you were "bargain-shopping;" your dollars purchased more assets at a reduced price. When you are in retirement, you are no longer the purchaser; you are selling. So, in a down market, you have to sell more assets to make the same amount of money as what you made in a favorable market.

I've had lots of people step into my office to talk to me about this, emphasizing, "my advisor says the market always bounces back, and I have to just hold on for the long term."

There's some basis for this thinking; thus far, the market has always rebounded to higher heights than before. But this is no guarantee, and the prospect of potentially higher returns in five years may not be very helpful in retirement if you are relying on the income from those returns to pay this month's electric bill, for example.

Is There a "Perfect" Product?

To bring us back around to the discussion of protection, growth, and liquidity, the ideal product would be a "ten" in all three categories, right? Completely guaranteed, doubling in size every few years, and accessible whenever you want. Does such a product exist? Absolutely not.

Instead of running in circles looking for that perfect product, the silver bullet, the unicorn of financial strategies, it's more important to circle back to the concept of a balanced, asset-diverse portfolio.

This is why your interests may be best served when you work with a trusted financial professional who knows what various financial products can do and how to use them in your personal retirement strategy.

*****

I think that a fundamental part of the financial advisor/client relationship is behavioral coaching. Market volatility can be an emotional trap that costs real money. There is a saying in our office that goes like this: "Emotion costs you money; discipline makes you money."

Pulling out of the market when it is falling can lock in losses and could lead to missing out on any subsequent rally.

When it comes to managing client behavior, especially in times of severe market volatility, I think about Dalbar. Since 1984, independent investment research firm Dalbar Inc. has published its annual Quantitative Analysis of Investor Behavior report, or QAIB.

This research series studies investor performance in mutual funds. Its goal is to shed light on how investors can improve portfolio performances by managing behaviors that cause them to act imprudently. And guess what?

Over the years, the set of longer-term data analyzed in these QAIB reports clearly shows that people are more often than not their own worst enemies when it comes to investing.

These conclusions were once again reaffirmed in the 2022 study: Investment results are more dependent on investor behavior than on fund performance. The most recent study found that fund investors who remained patient and didn't focus on short-term market gyrations were significantly more successful than those who let their emotions override a longer-term strategy to build wealth.

As the study implies, we find that a comprehensive financial plan is only as good as an investor's ability to stick to it through thick and thin. We find that constant communication is a big factor in managing emotion in the sphere of managing risk, whether markets are in turmoil or not. After all, we try to help our clients achieve long-term goals and live a lifestyle they deserve. We manage through periods of market volatility.

Sometimes, this can mean playing defense. Let me explain.

The fuel that drives your retirement lifestyle is income.

Without income, it becomes very difficult to achieve goals, let alone live a desired lifestyle. How do we set about doing this, particularly in periods of market volatility?

We typically help our clients play defense and gain protection in their retirement planning following a certain principle we view as fundamental.

You want to make sure that you don't have too much of your income tied to the ups and downs of the market. Income is the key to a secure and enjoyable retirement. It is difficult to have a good time if you are always worried about the stability of your retirement income.

One way to do this is to divide the income stream into two buckets. The first is what you might call the essential income bucket—those critical sources that finance your day-to-day lifestyle. The second is a long-term bucket—consider these sources to be residual, the remaining portion of your income that is not needed immediately.

By starting with income, you can build a plan that is able to absorb the shocks of the kinds of market volatility that we have seen over the last two years, which were most acutely felt when the pandemic was in its earliest stages.

Market volatility is a market reality. Managing through it and navigating around it is a retirement planning necessity today.

CHAPTER 4

Retirement Income

Retirement. For many of us, it's what we've saved for and dreamed of, pinning our hopes to a magical someday. Is that someday full of traveling? Is it filled with grandkids? Gardening? Maybe your fondest dream is simply never having to work again, never having to clock in or be accountable to someone else.

Your ability to do these things all hinges on *income*. Without the money to support these dreams, even a basic level of work-free lifestyle is unsustainable. That's why planning for your income in retirement is so foundational. But where do we begin?

It's easy to feel overwhelmed by this question. Some may feel the urge to amass a large lump sum and then try to put it all in one product—insurance, investments, liquid assets—to provide all the growth, liquidity, and income they need. Instead, I think you need a more balanced approach. After all, retirement planning isn't magic. Like I mention elsewhere, there is no single product that can be all things to all people (or even all things to one person). No approach works unilaterally for everyone. That's why it's important to talk to a financial professional who can help you lay down the basics and take you step-by-step through the process. Not only will you have the assurance you have addressed the areas you need to, but you also will have an ally who can help you break down the process and help keep you from feeling overwhelmed.

Sources of Income

Thinking of all the pieces of your retirement expenses might be intimidating. But, like cleaning out a junk drawer or revisiting that garage remodel, once you have laid everything out, you can begin to sort things into categories.

Once you have a good overall picture of where your expenses will lie, you can start stacking up the resources to cover them.

Social Security

Social Security is a guaranteed, inflation-protected federal insurance program playing a significant part in most of our retirement plans. From delaying until you've reached full retirement age or beyond to examining spousal benefits, as I discuss elsewhere in this book, there is plenty you can do to try to make the most of this monthly benefit. As with all your retirement income sources, it's important to consider how to make this resource stretch to provide the most bang and buck for your situation.

Pension

Another generally reliable source of retirement income for you might be a pension, if you are one of the lucky people who still has one.

If you don't have a pension, go ahead and skim on to the next section. If you do have a pension, keep on reading.

Because your pension can be such a central piece of your retirement income plan, you will want to put some thought into answering basic questions about it.

How well is your pension funded? Since the heyday of the pension plan, companies and governments have neglected to fund their pension obligations, causing a persistent problem with this otherwise reliable asset. However, research conducted by the Pew Charitable Trusts showed a collective increase in assets exceeding half a trillion dollars in state retirement plans fueled by strong market investment returns in fiscal 2021. Pew's estimates that state retirement systems rose to 80 percent funding for the first time in 2008.[23]

Consider the factors at play, though. Pensions had been underfunded and gained a boost from strong market performance in 2021. What happens to the solvency of those pension funds if the market declines?

It can be worthwhile to keep tabs on your pension's health and know what your options are for withdrawing your pension. If you have already retired and made those decisions, this may be a foregone conclusion. If not, it pays to know what you can expect and what decisions you can make, such as taking spousal options to cover your husband or wife if he or she outlives you.

Also, some companies are incentivizing lump-sum payouts of pensions to reduce the companies' payment liabilities. If that's the case with your employer, talk to your financial professional to see if it might be prudent to do something like that or if it might be better to stick with lifetime payments or other options.

Your 401(k) and IRA

One "modern way" to save for retirement is in a 401(k) or IRA (or their nonprofit or governmental equivalents). These tax-advantaged accounts are, in my opinion, a poor substitute for pensions, but one of the biggest disservices we do to ourselves is to not take full advantage of them in the first place. According to one article, only 41 percent of Americans invest in a 401(k), though 68 percent of employed Americans have access to a 401(k)-benefit option.[24]

Also, if you have changed jobs over the years, do the work of tracking down any benefits from your past employers. You might

---

[23] pewtrusts.org. September 14, 2021. "The State Pension Funding Gap: Plans Have Stabilized in Wake of Pandemic." https://www.pewtrusts.org/en/research-and-analysis/issue-briefs/2021/09/the-state-pension-funding-gap-plans-have-stabilized-in-wake-of-pandemic

[24] Amin Dabit. personalcapital.com. April 1, 2021. "The Average 401k Balance by Age." https://www.personalcapital.com/blog/retirement-planning/average-401k-balance-age/

have an IRA here or a 401(k) there; keep track of those so you can pull them together and look at those assets when you're ready to look at establishing sources of retirement income.

Do You Have...

- Life insurance?
- Annuities?
- Long-term care insurance?
- Any passive income sources?
- Stock and bond portfolios?
- Liquid assets? (What's in your bank account?)
- Alternative investments?
- Rental properties?

If you are going through the work of sitting with a financial professional, it's important to look at your full retirement income picture and pull together *all* your assets, no matter how big or small. From the free insurance policy offered at your bank to the sizable investment in your brother-in-law's modestly successful furniture store, you want to have a good idea of where your money is.

Let me introduce you to Brian. His story is central to what we do.

Brian is sixty-seven years of age and plans on fully retiring in eight years. He has saved close to $1 million in retirement accounts including simplified employee pension plan (SEP), traditional IRAs and his current 401(k). When we first met with him in 2021, Brian was nervous about the stock market and was mostly in cash. He was considering some strategies to minimize taxes, including a Roth conversion strategy, and wanted to work with a financial advisor that had the tools to present bottom line pros and cons of different scenarios. Brian's wife collects a pension from her work in the public school system. The couple collects Social Security, and they have no major liabilities like large credit card balances and mortgages. The couple has two adult children that do well in their own right, and legacy is not a huge concern.

Brian had a very good handle on his projected retirement expenses, and he had already crunched some numbers by performing a retirement income analysis of his own. Brian came to us knowing "he and his wife would be okay in retirement."

Brian was super focused on retirement income. His bottom line was that he wanted to double his money in seven to ten years while focusing on capital preservation. Given his age and time horizon, it was an ambitious goal. More risk equals more return. That's the gut check for the client—they need to ask themselves, "am I willing to accept downside risk?" If the answer is no, then trade-offs need to be made in the form of sacrificing some upside. In retirement we're managing the downside potential as much as the upside. So we worked with him to help him achieve his goals.

As an independent registered investment advisor, we fulfill our fiduciary responsibility to our clients by presenting them with a full universe of institutional investment managers—it is important to note that we are not beholden to any one manager or fund family. Once we know that targeted rate of return, we present the client with 1-3 managers with best-in-class investment returns.

Brian had a 10-year timeframe and an appetite for a moderate level of risk in order to achieve his targeted 7.0 percent rate of return (a rate that was determined based on his time horizon and age).

Most of our clients want to know the "why" behind moves that are being made within their accounts. That is why it important to us (as a firm) that we partner with investment managers that share their forecast for the markets at home and abroad. We have a firm understanding of why investment changes are being made in the portfolio, and we can communicate that to our clients during our quarterly calls and annual review meetings. Our clients appreciate that level of transparent communication.

Being able to offer clients that level of color commentary provides clients with peace of mind, greater control over their portfolio and offers enhanced ability to manage downside risk.

Brian ultimately chose to dollar cost average from his sizable cash position into a moderate growth model. Dollar cost averaging is the practice of investing a fixed dollar amount on a regular basis, regardless of the share price. It's a good way to develop a disciplined investing habit, allows you to be more efficient in how you invest and potentially lowers your stress level in volatile markets like the one we're in.

Brian ultimately paused his plans to "leg into" the moderate growth model as his worst fears about the health of the market came to fruition in the first quarter of 2022.

The model performed well between August to December of 2021. Then the rocky start to 2022 gave Brian the motivation to pause his programmatic investment plan. Notably, that is one of the benefits of not committing all your cash all at once.

During a review with Brian, there was a shift in the strategy based on how the market is behaving.

Part of the job of a financial professional is to present clients with fresh ideas based on what we see in the markets. Sometimes the best course of action is to ride out the storm (and we make the case as to why). Other times, there may be significant imbalances in the market that we want to take advantage of—as long as the client's risk tolerance and time horizon are intact and there is opportunity to maintain upside while managing downside risk.

In Brian's case, he is "glass half empty" when it comes to the market. His gut tells him things will get worse before they get better.

We presented options for him to consider that work well in a challenging and uncertain environment. Brian is on his way to achieving his goals.

There are a couple of key lessons here. Planning is important, but plans can change over time. In this instance, the client wanted to double his money in a stated period of time, so it was about growing his wealth which, in turn, would grow his retirement income. Brian is off to a good start. We believe this is the case because of the open communication between the financial advisors and the client; it's a collaborative effort. Furthermore, the scope, direction, long-term objective, and implementation in this example are dependent on working within a process. I address process in subsequent pages.

Good decisions today pay off for years and years to come.

Retirement Income Needs

How much income will you need in retirement? How do you determine that? A lot of people work toward a random number, thinking, "If I can just have a million dollars, I'll be comfortable in retirement!" Don't get me wrong; it is possible to save up a lot of money and then retire in the hopes you can keep your monthly expenses lower than some set estimation. But I think this carries a general risk of running out of money. Instead, we work with our clients to find out what their current and projected income needs are and then work from there to see how we might cover any gaps between what they have and what they want.

Goals and Dreams

I like to start with your pie in the sky. Do you find yourself planning for your vacations more thoroughly than you do your retirement? It's not uncommon for Americans to spend more time planning our vacations than we spend planning our retirements. Maybe it's because planning a vacation is less stressful: Having a week at the beach go awry is, well, a walk on the beach compared to running out of money in retirement. Whatever the case, perhaps it would be better if you thought of your retirement as a vacation in and of itself—no clocking in, no boss, no overtime. If you felt unlimited by financial strain, what would you do?

Would an endless vacation for you mean Paris and Rome? Would it mean mentoring at children's clubs or serving at the local soup kitchen? Or maybe it would mean deepening your ties to those immediately around you—neighbors, friends, and family. Maybe it would mean more time to take part in the hobbies and activities you love. Have you been considering a second (or even third) act as a small-business owner, turning a hobby or passion into a revenue source?

This is your time to daydream and answer the question: If you could do anything, what would you do?

After that, it's a matter of putting a dollar amount on it. What are the costs of round-the-world travel? One couple I know said their highest priority in retirement was being able to take each of their grandchildren on a cross-country vacation every year. That's a pretty specific goal—one that is reasonably easy to nail down a budget for.

Current Budget

Compiling a current expense report is one of the trickiest pieces of retirement preparation. Many people assume the expenses of their lives in retirement will be different—lower. After all, there will be no drive to work, no need for a formal wardrobe, and, perhaps most impactful of all, no more saving for retirement!

Yet, we often underestimate our daily spending habits. That's why we typically ask our clients to bring in their bank statements for the past year—they are reflective of your *actual* spending, not just what you think you're spending.

Our advisors can't count the number of times they have sat with a couple, asked them about their spending, and heard them throw out a number that seemed incredibly low. When we ask them where the number came from, they usually say they estimated based on their total bills. Yet, our spending is so much more than our mortgage, utilities, cable, phone, car, grocery, or credit card bills.

"What about clothes?" I ask, "Or dining out? What about gifts and coffees and last-minute birthday cards?" That's when the lights come on.

This is why I suggest collecting a year's worth of information. There is usually no such thing as a one-time purchase. Did you buy new furniture? Even if that is a rarity, do you think that will be the last time you *ever* buy furniture?

Another hefty expense is spending on the kids. Many of the couples we work with are quick to help their adult children, whether it's something like letting them live in the basement, paying for college, babysitting, paying an occasional bill, or contributing to a grandchild's college fund. Research concluded that 22 percent of adults receive some kind of financial support from parents. That segment jumps to almost 30 percent when factoring the generation we call millennials.[25]

---

[25] Kamaron McNair. magnifymoney.com. October 26, 2021. "Nearly 30% of Millenials Still Receive Financial Support From Their Parents." https://www.magnifymoney.com/blog/news/parental-financial-support-survey/

My clients sometimes protest that what they do for their grown children can stop in retirement. They don't *need* to help. But I get it. Parents like to feel needed. And, while you never want to neglect saving for retirement in favor of taking on financial risks (like your child's student debt), the parents who help their adult children do so in part because it helps them feel fulfilled.

When it comes down to expenses, including (and especially) spending on your family, don't make your initial calculations based on what you *could* whittle your budget down to if you *had* to. Instead, start from where you are. Who wants to live off a bare-bones bank account in retirement?

Other Expenses

Once you have nailed down your current budget and your dreams or goals for retirement, there are a few other outstanding pieces to think about—some expenses many people don't take the time to consider before making and executing a plan. But I'm assuming you want to get it right, so let's take a look.

Housing

Do you know where you want to live in retirement? This makes up a substantial piece of your income puzzle—since the typical American household owns a home, and it's generally their largest asset.

Some people prefer to live right where they are for as long as they can. Others have been waiting for retirement to pull the trigger on an ambitious move, like purchasing a new house, or even downsizing. Whatever your plans and whatever your reasons, there are quite a few things to consider.

Mortgage
Do you still have a mortgage? What may have been a nice tax boon in your working years could turn into a financial burden in your retirement. After all, when you are on a limited income, a mortgage

is just one more bill sapping your financial strength. It is something to put some thought into, whether you plan to age in place or are considering moving to your dream home, buying a house out of state, or living in a retirement community.

Upkeep and Taxes

A house without a mortgage still requires annual taxes. While it's tempting to think of this as a once-a-year expense, when you have limited earning potential, your annual tax bill might be something into which you should put a little more forethought.

The costs of homeownership aren't just monetary. When you find yourself dealing with more house than you need, it can drain your time and energy. From keeping clutter at bay to keeping the lawn mower running, upkeep can be extensive and expensive. For some, that's a challenge they heartily accept and can comfortably take on. For others, the idea of yard work or cleaning an area larger than they need feels foolish.

For instance, Peggy discovered after her knee replacement that most of her house was inaccessible to her when she was laid up: "It felt ridiculous to pay someone else to dust and vacuum a house I was only living in 40 percent of!"

Practicality and Adaptability

Erik and Magda are looking to retire within the next two decades. They just sold their old three-bedroom ranch-style house. Their twins are in high school, and the couple has wanted to "upgrade" for years. Now they live in a gorgeous 1940s three-story house with all the kitchen space they ever wanted, five sprawling bedrooms, and a library and media room for themselves and their children. Within months of moving in, the couple realized a house perfect for their active teens would no longer be perfect for them in five to fifteen years.

"We are paying the mortgage for this house, but we've started saving for the next one," said Magda, "because who wants to climb two flights of stairs to their bedroom when they're seventy-eight?"

Others I know have encountered a similar situation in their personal lives. After a health crisis, one couple found the luxurious tub for two they toiled to install had become a specter of a bad slip and a potential safety risk. It's important to think through what your physical reality could be. I always emphasize to my clients that they should plan for whatever their long-term future might hold, but it's amazing how many people don't give it much thought.

Contracts and Regulations

If you are looking into a cross-country move, be aware of new tax tables or local ordinances in the area where you are looking to move. After all, you don't want to experience sticker-shock when you are looking at downsizing or reducing your bills in retirement.

Along the same lines, if you are moving into a retirement community, be sure to look at the fine print. What happens if you must move into a different situation for long-term care? Will you be penalized? Will you be responsible for replacing your slot in the community? What are all the fees, and what do they cover?

Inflation

As I write this in 2022, America has experienced a wave of inflation following a lengthy period of low inflation. Inflation zoomed to 8.5 percent in March 2022, a level not reached since 1981, and stood at 8.3 percent in April 2022.[26]

Core inflation is yet another measurement that excludes goods with prices that tend to be more volatile, such as food and energy costs. Core inflation for a 12-month period ending in April 2022 was 6.2 percent. It so happened energy prices rose a whopping 30.3 percent over that timeframe.[27]

---

[26] tradingeconomics.com. April 2022. "United States Inflation Rate."
https://tradingeconomics.com/united-states/inflation-cpi
[27] U.S. Inflation Calculator. "United States Core Inflation Rates (1957-2022)."
https://www.usinflationcalculator.com/inflation/united-states-core-inflation-rates/

However, inflation isn't a one-time bump; it has a cumulative effect. Again, that can impact the price of groceries greater than other goods. Even with relatively low inflation over the past few decades, an item you bought in 1997 for two dollars will cost $3.60 today.[28] Want to go to a show? A $20 ticket in 1997 would cost $40.34 in 2022.[29]

What if, in retirement, we hit a stretch like the late 1970s and early 1980s when annual inflation rates of 10 percent became the norm? It may be wise to consider some extra padding in your retirement income plan to account for any potential increase in inflation in the future.

Aging

Also, in the expense category, think about longevity. We all hope to age gracefully. However, it's important to face the prospect of aging with a sense of realism.

The elephant in the room for many families is long-term care. No one wants to admit they will likely need it, but estimates indicate almost 70 percent of us will.[30] Aging is a significant piece of retirement income planning because you'll want to figure out how to set aside money for your care, either at home or away from it. The more comfortable you get with discussing your wishes and plans with your loved ones, the easier planning for the financial side of it can be.

I denote health care and potential long-term care costs in more detail elsewhere in this book, but suffice it to say nursing home care tends to be very expensive and typically isn't something you get to choose when you will need.

It isn't just the costs of long-term care that pose a concern in living longer. It's also about covering the possible costs of everything else

---

[28] Ibid.

[29] In2013dollars.com "Admission to movies, theaters, and concerts priced at $20 in 1997>$40.34 in 2022." https://www.in2013dollars.com/Admission-to-movies,-theaters,-and-concerts/price-inflation

[30] Moll Law Group. 2022. "The Cost of Long-Term Care." https://www.molllawgroup.com/the-cost-of-long-term-care.html

associated with living longer. For instance, if Henry retires from his job as a biochemical engineer at age sixty-five, perhaps he planned to have a very decent income for twenty years, until age eighty-five. But what if he lives until he's ninety-five? That's a whole third—ten years—more of personal income he will need.

Putting It All Together

Whew! So, you have pulled together what you have, and you have a pretty good idea of where you want to be. Now your financial professional and you can go about the work of arranging what assets you *have* to cover what you *need*—and how you might try to cover any gaps.

Like the proverbial man in the Bible who built his house on a rock, I like to help my clients figure out how to cover their day-to-day living expenses—their needs—with insurance and other guaranteed income sources like pensions and Social Security.

At Kelly Financial Services we employ a process that is called "Safe Money Strategies.™"

Today, the kinds of discussions the advisors at Kelly Financial Services LLC are having with our clients center around goals and lifestyles, not just market returns. It is a better way to get to what is really important to you.

The approach is defined by two key factors: financial planning is *holistic*, and it is a *process*. These two attributes are useful for clients and planners alike. A holistic approach helps identify goals and a process helps achieve them.

Embracing a process will not guarantee that you will achieve your goals or live a desired lifestyle. But you will have a greater probability of success by using a process. Our process involves five steps: discover, analyze, develop, implement, and review. Our process can be defined by two crucial characteristics. One, it is immersive. It is designed to engage clients and with constant communication it compels engagement and thus, it becomes an immersive experience. And two, while the process is ongoing and cyclical, it is flexible enough to not only allow for change in plans, it helps identify when changes to plans should be made.

Again, you should keep in mind there isn't one single financial vehicle, asset, or source to fill all your needs, and that's okay. One of the challenges of planning for your income in retirement concerns figuring out what products and strategies to use. You can release some of that stress when you accept the fact you will probably need a diverse portfolio—potentially with bonds, stocks, insurance, and other income sources—not just one massive money pile.

One way to help shore up your income gaps is by working with your financial professional and a qualified tax advisor to mitigate your tax exposure. If you have a 401(k) or IRA, a tax advisor in your corner can help you figure out how and when to take distributions from your account in a way that doesn't push you into a higher tax bracket. Or you might learn how to use tax-advantaged bonds more effectively. Effective tax planning isn't necessarily about "adding" to your income. Especially regarding retirement, it's less about what you make than it is about what you keep. Paying a lower tax bill keeps more money in your pocket, which is where you want it when it comes to retirement income.

Now you can look at ways to cover your remaining retirement goals. Are there products like long-term care insurance specific to a certain kind of expense you anticipate? Is there a particular asset you want to use for your "play" money—money for trips and gifts for the grandkids? Is there any way you can portion off money for those charitable legacy plans?

Once you have analyzed your income wants, needs, and the assets to realistically cover them, you may have a gap. The masterstroke of a competent financial professional will be to help you figure out how you will cover that gap. Will you need to cut out a round of golf a week? Maybe skip the new car? Or will you need to take more substantial action?

One way to cover an income gap is to consider working longer or even part-time before retirement and even after that magical calendar date. This may not be the best "plan" for you; disabilities, work demands, and physical or emotional limitations can hinder the best-laid plans to continue working. However, if it is physically possible for you, this is one considerable way to help your assets last, for more than one reason.

In fact, 46 percent of the Americans responding to a survey report they plan to work part-time after retiring, while 18 percent indicated they planned to work past the age of seventy.[31]

I think it is fair to say that when people look to work with a financial professional for retirement advice, they seek answers to three fundamental questions: Will I have enough to retire? When can I retire? Will my family be okay if something happens to me?

I think it is also fair to say that most prospective clients working with us fall into three categories.

In the first category are those people who are well prepared: They have the savings and income streams and have plans in place; they need help more with the preservation and distribution of wealth than the generation of wealth. The second group has done an adequate job of preparing for retirement. They likely will require more assistance with the generation of income than the above group of people. But they are well on their way. The third category involves people with significant deficiencies, principally on the income generation side of things—which clearly affects the preservation and distribution of wealth later in life. Depending on their long-term goals, they might need to dramatically increase savings, reduce debt, and work longer.

We have worked with all three types of clients. I don't want to discourage people from seeking the advice of a financial professional, especially if you find yourself in the last category. Getting a second opinion on your future finances is just as important as getting a second opinion on a medical diagnosis that could impact your future, too. No matter where you find yourself on the spectrum, it is important to start planning and saving sometime, preferably as early as possible.

---

[31] Palash Ghosh. Forbes.com. May 6, 2021. "A Third Of Seniors Seek To Work Well Past Retirement Age, Or Won't Retire At All, Poll Finds."
https://www.forbes.com/sites/palashghosh/2021/05/06/a-third-of-seniors-seek-to-work-well-past-retirement-age-or-wont-retire-at-all-poll-finds/?sh=1d2ece836b95

Still, we share the joy of those prospects who do meet with us, and they find themselves fully prepared for retirement. Part of my mission at Kelly Financial, via education and public services, is to get as many people as possible into this first category.

When you're retired, you no longer have an employer paying you a steady check. It is up to you to make sure you have saved and planned for the income you need.

CHAPTER 5

Social Security

S ocial Security is often the foundation of retirement income. Backed by the strength of the U.S. Treasury, it provides perhaps the most dependable paycheck you will have in retirement.

From the time you collect your first paycheck from the job that made you a bona fide taxpayer (for me, it was working at my family's John Deere dealership down in Georgia), you are paying into the grand old Social Security system. What grew and developed out of the pressures of the Great Depression has become one of the most popular government programs in the country, and, if you pay in for the equivalent of ten years or more, you, too, can benefit from the Social Security program.

At Kelly Financial, we take a step back before we take a step forward with our clients.

What do I mean by this? Before we enter into any serious Social Security discussions with clients, we simply step back to listen and learn from them. We want to hear from them about what their retirement looks like, how they envision their lifestyle. We want to know about their sources of income and their health, among other things.

A clearer picture then emerges. We are able to formulate a strategy and unlock all the benefits for Social Security as part of the larger plan. This is where the steps go forward.

Now, before we get into the nitty-gritty of Social Security, I'd like to address a current concern: Will Social Security still be there for you when you reach retirement age?

The Future of Social Security

This question is ever-present as headlines trumpet an underfunded Social Security program, alongside the sea of baby boomers retiring in droves and the comparatively smaller pool of younger people who are funding the system.

The Social Security Administration itself acknowledges this concern as each Social Security statement now bears an asterisk that continues near the end of the summary:

> *"*Your estimated benefits are based on current law. Congress has made changes to the law in the past and can do so at any time. The law governing benefit amounts may change because, by 2034, the payroll taxes collected will be enough to pay only about 79 percent of scheduled benefits."*

Just a reminder, as if you needed one, that nothing in life is guaranteed. Additionally, depending on who you're listening to, Social Security funds may run low before 2034 thanks to the financial instability and government spending that accompanied the 2020 COVID-19 pandemic.

Before you get too discouraged, though, here are a few thoughts to keep you going:

- Even if the program is only paying 79 cents on the dollar for scheduled benefits, 79 percent is notably not zero.
- The Social Security Administration has made changes in the distant and near past to protect the fund's solvency, including increasing retirement ages and striking certain filing strategies.
- There are many changes Congress could make, and lawmakers routinely discuss how to fix the system, such as further increasing full retirement age and eligibility.
- One thing no one is seriously discussing: Reneging on current obligations to retirees or the soon-to-retire.

Take heart. The real answer to the question, "Will Social Security be there for me?" is still yes.

This question is important to consider when you look at how much we, as a nation, rely on this program. Did you know Social Security benefits replace about 40 percent of a person's original income when they retire?[32]

If you ask me, that's a pretty significant piece of your retirement income puzzle.

Another caveat? You may not realize this, but no one can legally "advise" you about your Social Security benefits.

"But, Kelly," you may be thinking, "isn't that part of what you do? And what about that nice gentleman at the Social Security Administration office I spoke with on the phone?"

Don't get me wrong. Social Security Administration employees know their stuff. They are trained to understand policies and programs, and they are usually pretty quick to tell you what you can and cannot do. But the government specifically stipulates, because Social Security is a benefit you alone have paid into and earned, your Social Security decisions, too, are yours alone.

When it comes to financial professionals, we can't push you in any direction, but—there's a big but here—working with a well-informed financial professional is still incredibly handy for your Social Security decisions. Why? Because someone who's worth his or her salt will know what withdrawal strategies might pertain to your specific situation and will ask questions that can help you determine what you are looking for when it comes to your Social Security.

For instance, some people want the highest possible monthly benefit. Others want to start their benefits early, not always because of financial need. I heard about one man who called in to start his Social Security payments the day he qualified, just because he liked to think of it as the government paying back a debt it owed him, and he enjoyed the feeling of receiving a check from Uncle Sam.

Whatever your reasons, questions, or feelings regarding Social Security, the decision is yours alone; but working with a financial

---

[32] ssa.gov. "Alternate Measure of Replacement Rates for Social Security Benefits and Retirement Income." https://www.ssa.gov/policy/docs/ssb/v68n2/v68n2p1.html.

professional can help you put your options in perspective by showing you—both with industry knowledge and with proprietary software or planning processes—where your benefits fit into your overall strategy for retirement income.

One reason the federal government doesn't allow for "advice" related to Social Security, I suspect, is so no one can profit from giving you advice related to your Social Security benefit—or from providing any clarifications. Again, this is a sign of a good financial professional. Those who are passionate about their work will be knowledgeable about what benefit strategies might be to your advantage and will happily share those possible options with you.

Full Retirement Age

When it comes to Social Security, it seems like many people only think so far as "yes." They don't take the time to understand the various options available. Instead, because it is common knowledge you can begin your benefits at age sixty-two, that's what many of us do. While more people are opting to delay taking benefits, age sixty-two is still firmly the most popular age to start.[33]

What many people fail to understand is, by starting benefits early, they may be leaving a lot of money on the table. You see, the Social Security Administration bases your monthly benefit on two factors: your earnings history and your full retirement age (FRA).

From your earnings history, they pull the thirty-five years you made the most money and use a mathematical indexing formula to figure out a monthly average from those years. If you paid into the system for less than thirty-five years, then every year you didn't pay in will be counted as a zero.

Once they have calculated what your monthly earning would be at FRA, the government then calculates what to put on your check based on how close you are to FRA. FRA was originally set at sixty-

---

[33] Chris Kissell. moneytalknews.com. January 20, 2021. "This Is When the Most People Start Taking Social Security." https://www.moneytalksnews.com/the-most-popular-age-for-claiming-social-security/

five, but, as the population aged and lifespans lengthened, the government shifted FRA later and later, based on an individual's year of birth. Check out this chart to see when you will reach FRA.[34]

Age to Receive Full Social Security Benefits*	
(Called "full retirement age" [FRA] or "normal retirement age.")	
Year of Birth*	**FRA**
1937 or earlier	65
1938	65 and 2 months
1939	65 and 4 months
1940	65 and 6 months
1941	65 and 8 months
1942	65 and 10 months
1943-1954	66
1955	66 and 2 months
1956	66 and 4 months
1957	66 and 6 months
1958	66 and 8 months
1959	66 and 10 months
1960 and later	67
If you were born on Jan. 1 of any year, you should refer to the previous year. (If you were born on the 1st of the month, we figure your benefit [and your full retirement age] as if your birthday was in the previous month.)	

34 Social Security Administration. "Full Retirement Age."
https://www.ssa.gov/planners/retire/retirechart.html

When you reach FRA, you are eligible to receive 100 percent of whatever the Social Security Administration says is your full monthly benefit.

Starting at age sixty-two, for every year before FRA you claim benefits, your monthly check is reduced by 5 percent or more. Conversely, for every year you delay taking benefits past FRA, your monthly benefit increases by 8 percent (until age seventy—after that, there is no monetary advantage to delaying Social Security benefits). While your circumstances and needs may vary, a lot of financial professionals still urge people to at least consider delaying until they reach age seventy.

Why wait?[35]

Taking benefits early could affect your monthly check by _____								
62	63	64	65	FRA 66	67	68	69	70
-25%	-20%	-13.3%	-6.7%	0	+8%	+16%	+24%	+32%

My Social Security

If you are over age thirty, you have probably received a notice from the Social Security Administration telling you to activate something called "My Social Security." This is a handy way to learn more about your particular benefit options, to keep track of what your earnings record looks like, and to calculate the benefits you have accrued over the years.

Essentially, My Social Security is an online account you can activate to see what your personal Social Security picture looks like, which you can do at www.ssa.gov/myaccount. This can be extremely helpful when it comes to planning for income in retirement and figuring up the difference between your anticipated income versus anticipated expenses.

---

[35] Social Security Administration. April 2021. "Can You Take Your Benefits Before Full Retirement Age?" https://www.ssa.gov/planners/retire/applying2.html

My Social Security is also helpful because it's a great way to see if there is a problem. For instance, I have heard of one woman who, through diligently checking her tax records against her Social Security profile, discovered her Social Security check was shortchanging her, based on her earnings history. After taking the discrepancy to the Social Security Administration, they sent her what they owed her in makeup benefits.

COLA

Social Security is a largely guaranteed piece of the retirement puzzle: If you get a statement that reads you should expect $1,000 a month, you can be sure you will receive $1,000 a month. But there is one variable detail, and that is something called the cost-of-living adjustment, or COLA.

The COLA is an increase in your monthly check meant to address inflation in everyday life. After all, your expenses likely will continue to experience inflation in retirement, but you will no longer have the opportunity for raises, bonuses, or promotions you had when you were working. Instead, Social Security receives an annual cost-of-living increase tied to the Department of Labor's Consumer Price Index for Urban Wage Earners and Clerical Workers, or CPI-W. If the CPI-W measurement shows inflation rose a certain amount for regular goods and services, then Social Security recipients will see that reflected in their COLA.

The COLA averages 4 percent, but in a no- or low-inflation environment, such as in 2010, 2011, and 2016, Social Security recipients will not receive an adjustment. Some view the COLA as a perk, bump, or bonus, but, in reality, it works more like this: Your mom sends you to the store with $2.50 for a gallon of milk. Milk costs exactly $2.50. The next week, you go back with that same amount, but it is now $2.52 for a gallon, so you go back to Mom, and she gives you 2 cents. You aren't bringing home more milk—it just costs more money.

So the COLA is less about "making more money" and more about keeping seniors' purchasing power from eroding when inflation is a big factor, such as in 1975, when it was 8 percent![36] Still, don't let that detract from your enthusiasm about COLAs; after all, what if Mom's solution was: "Here's the same $2.50; try to find pennies from somewhere else to get that milk!"?

Spousal Benefits

We've talked about FRA, but another big Social Security decision involves spousal benefits.

If you or your spouse has a long stretch of zeros in your earnings history—perhaps if one of you stayed home for years, caring for children or sick relatives—you may want to consider filing for spousal benefits instead of filing on your own earnings history. A spousal benefit can be up to 50 percent of the primary wage earner's benefit at full retirement age.

To begin drawing a spousal benefit, you must be at least sixty-two years old, and the primary wage earner must have already filed for his or her benefit. While there are penalties for taking spousal benefits early (you could lose up to 67.5 percent of your check for filing at age sixty-two), you cannot earn credits for delaying past full retirement age.[37]

Like I wrote, the spousal benefit can be a big deal for those who don't have a very long pay history, but it's important to weigh your own earned benefits against the option of withdrawing based on a fraction of your spouse's benefits.

To look at how this could play out, let's use a hypothetical couple: Mary Jane, who is sixty, and Peter, who is sixty-two.

Let's say Peter's benefit at FRA, in his case sixty-six, would be $1,600. If Peter begins his benefits right now, four years before FRA, his monthly check will be $1,200. If Mary Jane begins taking spousal benefits in two years at the earliest date possible, her monthly benefits

---

[36] Social Security Administration. "Cost-Of-Living Adjustment (COLA) Information for 2022." https://www.ssa.gov/cola/

[37] Social Security Administration. "Retirement Planner: Benefits For You As A Spouse." https://www.ssa.gov/planners/retire/applying6.html

will be reduced by 67.5 percent, to $520 per month (remember, at FRA, the most she can qualify for is half of Peter's FRA benefit).

What if Peter and Mary Jane both wait until FRA? At sixty-six, Peter begins taking his full benefit of $1,600 a month. Two years later, when she reaches age sixty-six, Mary Jane will qualify for $800 a month. By waiting until FRA, the couple's monthly benefit goes from $1,720 to $2,400.

What if Peter delays until age seventy to get his maximum possible benefit? For each year past FRA he delays, his monthly benefits increase by 8 percent. This means, at seventy, he could file for a monthly benefit of $2,176. However, delayed retirement credits do not affect spousal benefits, so as soon as Peter files at seventy, Mary Jane also would file (at age sixty-eight) for her maximum benefit of $800, so their highest possible combined monthly check is $2,976.[38]

When it comes to your Social Security benefits, you obviously will want to consider whether a monthly check based on a fraction of your spouse's earnings will be comparable to or larger than your own earnings history.

Divorced Spouses

There are a few considerations for those of us who have gone through a divorce. If you 1) were married for ten years or more *and* 2) since have been divorced for at least two years *and* 3) are unmarried *and* 4) your ex-spouse qualifies to begin Social Security, you qualify for a spousal benefit based on your ex-husband or ex-wife's earnings history at FRA. A divorced spousal benefit is different from the married spousal benefit in one way: You don't have to wait for your ex-spouse to file before you can file yourself.[39]

For instance, Charles and Moira were married for fifteen years before their divorce, when he was thirty-six and she was forty. Moira

---

[38] Office of the Chief Actuary. Social Security Administration. "Social Security Benefits: Benefits for Spouses." https://www.ssa.gov/oact/quickcalc/spouse.html
[39] Social Security Administration. "Retirement Planner: If You Are Divorced." https://www.ssa.gov/planners/retire/divspouse.html

has been remarried for twenty years, and, although Charles briefly remarried, his second marriage ended after a few years. Charles' benefits are largely calculated based on his many years of volunteering in schools, meaning his personal monthly benefit is close to zero.

Although Moira has deferred her retirement, opting to delay benefits until she is seventy, Charles can begin taking benefits calculated from Moira's work history at FRA as early as sixty-two. However, he also will have the option of waiting until FRA to collect the maximum, or 50 percent of Moira's earned monthly benefit at her FRA.

Widowed Spouses

If your marriage ended with the death of your spouse, you might claim a benefit for your spouse's earned income as his or her widow/widower, called a survivor's benefit. Unlike a spousal benefit or divorced benefits, if your husband or wife dies, you can claim his or her full benefit. Also, unlike spousal benefits, if you need to, you can begin taking income when you turn sixty. However, as with other benefit options, your monthly check will be permanently reduced for withdrawing benefits before FRA.

If your spouse began taking benefits before he or she died, you can't delay withdrawing your survivor's benefits to get delayed credits. The Social Security Administration maintains you can only get as much from a survivor's benefit as your deceased spouse might have received, had he or she lived.[40]

Taxes, Taxes, Taxes

With Social Security, as with everything, it is important to consider taxes. It may be surprising, but your Social Security benefits are not tax-free. Despite having been taxed to accrue those benefits in the

---

[40] Social Security Administration. "Social Security Benefit Amounts For The Surviving Spouse By Year Of Birth."
https://www.ssa.gov/planners/survivors/survivorchartred.html

first place, you may have to pay Uncle Sam income taxes on up to 85 percent of your Social Security.

The Social Security Administration figures these taxes using what they call "the provisional income formula." Your provisional income formula differs from the adjusted gross income you use for your regular income taxes. Instead, to find out how much of your Social Security benefit is taxable, the Social Security Administration calculates it this way:

Provisional Income = Adjusted Gross Income + Nontaxable Interest + ½ of Social Security

See that piece about nontaxable interest? That generally means interest from government bonds and notes. It surprises many people that, although you may not pay taxes on those assets, their income will count against you when it comes to Social Security taxation.

Once you have figured out your provisional income (also called "combined income"), you can use the following chart to figure out your Social Security taxes.[41]

---

[41] Social Security Administration. "Benefits Planner: Income Taxes and Your Social Security Benefits." https://www.ssa.gov/planners/taxes.html

Taxes on Social Security		
Provisional Income = Adjusted Gross Income + Nontaxable Interest + ½ of Social Security		
If you are ____ and your provisional income is____, then...		Uncle Sam will tax ___ of your Social Security
Single	Married, filing jointly	
Less than $25,000	Less than $32,000	0%
$25,000 to $34,000	$32,000 to $44,000	Up to 50%
More than $34,000	More than $44,000	Up to 85%

This is one more reason it may benefit you to work with financial and tax professionals. They can look at your entire financial picture to make your overall retirement plan as tax-efficient as possible—including your Social Security benefit.

Working and Social Security: The Earnings Test

If you haven't reached FRA, but you started your Social Security benefits and are still working, things get a little hairy.

Because you have started Social Security payments, the Social Security Administration will pay out your benefits (at that reduced rate, of course, because you haven't reached your FRA). Yet, because you are working, the organization also must withhold from your check to add to your benefits, which you are already collecting. See how this complicates matters?

To address the situation, the government has what is called the earnings test. For 2022, you can earn up to $19,560 without it affecting your Social Security check. But, for every $2 you earn past that amount, the Social Security Administration will withhold $1. The earnings test loosens in the year of your FRA; if you are reaching FRA in 2022, you can earn up to $51,960 before you run into the earnings test, and the government only withholds $1 for every $3 past that amount. The month you reach FRA, you are no longer subject to any earnings withholding. For instance, if you are still working and will turn sixty-six on December 28, 2022, you would only have to worry about the earnings test until December, and then you can ignore it entirely. Keep in mind, the money the government withholds from your Social Security benefits while you are working before FRA will be tacked back onto your benefits check after FRA.[42]

It is easy to get lost in the minutia of Social Security.

There are so many variables that it reminds me of all of those Rubik's Cube combinations when it first came out in the 1980s. I suppose that is a good analogy for solving the Social Security puzzle, too. But unlike those whizzes who can solve a Rubik's Cube in seconds flat, planning Social Security for people is different. It requires time and thought.

It might make sense to take a step back and view the forest before the trees. We keep in mind three basic rules when advising clients on Social Security. We think this brings a fresh perspective and allows a sharper focus on a subject that can easily lose people in the forest.

Of course, one's health, longevity, and cash flows are always factors that impact these three rules. The three rules are as follows:

#1: Patience pays. You can take benefits starting at age sixty-two. Remember, though, that every year that you wait, Social Security will pay you a benefit that is 8 percent higher than the year before. Notably, 44 percent of people claim benefits early, at age sixty-two. The longer you can wait, the bigger the payoff.

---

[42] Social Security Administration. "Exempt Amounts Under the Earnings Test." https://www.ssa.gov/oact/cola/rtea.html

#2: <u>Take all you can get</u>. Know about all the available benefits. A financial professional should be able to help you identify them, weigh all the variables, and help you decide the best time to claim your benefits, as well as the type of your benefits. It is estimated that 90 percent of all Social Security recipients leave money on the table.

#3: <u>Timing is everything</u>. Simply stated, the success of something is often related to when it happens.

CHAPTER 6

401(k)s & IRAs

Have you heard? Today's retirement is not your parents' retirement. You see, back in the day, it was pretty common to work for one company for the vast majority of your career and then retire with a gold watch and a pension.

The gold watch was a symbol of the quality time you had put in at that company, but the pension was more than a symbol. Instead, it was a guarantee—as solid as your employer—that they would repay your hard work with a certain amount of income in your old age. Did you see the caveat there? Your pension's guarantee was *as solid as your employer*. The problem was, what if your employer went under?

Companies that failed couldn't pay their retired employees' pensions, leading to financial challenges for many. Beginning in 1974 with Congress' passage of the Employee Retirement Income Security Act, federal legislation and regulations aimed at protecting retirees were everywhere. One piece of legislation included a relatively obscure section of the Internal Revenue Code, added in 1978. Section 401(k), to be specific.

IRC section 401, subsection k, created tax advantages for employer-sponsored financial products, even if the main contributor was the employee him or herself. Over the years, more employers took note, beginning an age of transition away from pensions and toward 401(k) plans. A 401(k) is a retirement account with certain tax benefits and restrictions on the investments or other financial products inside of it.

Essentially, 401(k)s and their individual retirement account (IRA) counterparts are "wrappers" that provide tax benefits around assets; typically, the assets that compose IRAs and 401(k)s are mutual funds, stock and bond mixes, and money market accounts. However, IRA and 401(k) contents are becoming more diverse these days, with some companies offering different kinds of annuity options within their plans.

Where pensions are defined-*benefit* plans, 401(k)s and IRAs are defined-*contribution* plans. The one-word change outlines the basic difference. Pensions spell out what you can expect to receive from the plan but not necessarily how much money it will take to fund those benefits. With 401(k)s, an employer sets a standard for how much they will contribute (if any), and you can be certain of what you are contributing. Still, there is no outline for what you can expect to receive in return for those contributions.

Modern employment looks very different. A 2020 survey by the Bureau of Labor Statistics determined U.S. workers stayed with their employers a median of 4.1 years. Workers ages fifty-five to sixty-four had a little more staying power and were most likely to stay with their employer for about ten years.[43] Participation in 401(k) plans has steadily risen this century, totaling $7.3 trillion in assets in 2021 compared to $3.1 trillion in 2011. About 60 million active participants engaged in 401(k) plans in 2020.[44]

Those statistics make it clear that 401(k) plans have replaced pensions at many companies and, for that matter, a gold watch.

New data to emerge suggest that planning for retirement with a pension is different from planning for a retirement without one, or a small one. And the big difference has to do with drawdown rates.

The Center for Retirement Research at Boston College recently released a brief on this very subject. The center's analysis found that households with a defined benefit plan—again, think traditional

---

[43] Bureau of Labor Statistics. September 22, 2020. "Employee Tenure Summary." https://www.bls.gov/news.release/tenure.nr0.htm
[44] Investment Company Institute. October 11, 2021. "Frequently Asked Questions About 401(k) Plan Research." https://www.ici.org/faqs/faq/401k/faqs_401k

pension—retain more of their wealth, that is they draw it down more slowly than those with a 401(k).

And consider this nugget from the center: A household retiring with $200,000 in savings and a defined benefit plan would retain $28,000 more wealth at age seventy than a similar household with no defined benefit plan. Furthermore, the analysis suggests that "many new retirees could deplete their 401(k) assets by age eighty-five, meaning that they face a greater risk of outliving their savings."

There is a cautionary tale here. Given all the changes in the retirement landscape, there are distinctions between the oldest boomers (those born roughly 1946-1953) and younger boomers (those born between 1960-1965).

The big difference today is that those older boomers mostly relied upon defined benefit retirement plans (think the old-school pension plan) for the bulk of their source of retirement money. Whereas the younger boomers have had to rely mostly on defined contribution plans (like 401(k)s). And more recent research suggests that those all-important drawdown rates differ between those who depend mostly on defined benefit plans from those who depend on defined contribution plans.

Forecasts for the younger boomers based on the drawdowns of past generations likely underestimate their drawdown speed.

As the center concludes, the results suggest that boomers without defined benefit plans may be drawing down their assets faster, leaving them with more risk that they will outlive their savings.

These changes should not be entirely surprising. A financial professional should recognize the new trends and address them with clients accordingly.

And one more note on pensions. Pensions are always a complicated conversation; it all depends on what the client is trying to accomplish.

We have had many conversations with clients where they will take the lump sum payout. The benefit of this is it provides the ability to pass assets on to the next generation. The drawback is that they will not get a steady stream of income throughout retirement.

In other conversations, the client has chosen to take an income stream. The income is good for someone who is looking for a steady stream of income to help with living expenses. The drawback is that when you take the income stream very rarely is the stream passed on to the next generation. It usually stops with the passing of the recipient and/or their spouse.

*****

If there is anything to learn from this paradigm shift, it's that you must look out for yourself. Whether you have worked for a company for two years or twenty, you are still the one who has to look out for your own best interests. That holds doubly true when it comes to preparing for retirement. If you are one of the lucky ones who still has a pension, good for you. But for the rest of us, it is likely a 401(k)—or possibly one of its nonprofit- or government-sector counterparts, a 403(b) or 457 plan—is one of your biggest assets for retirement.

Some employers offer incentives to contribute to their company plans, like a company match. On that subject, I have one thing to say: *Do it!* Nothing in life is free, as they say, but a company match on your retirement funds is about as close to free money as it gets. If you can make the minimum to qualify for your company's match at all, go for it.

Now, it's likely, during our working years, we mostly "set and forget" our 401(k) funding. Because it is tax-advantaged, your employer is taking money from your paycheck—before taxes—and putting it into your plan for you. Maybe you got to pick a selection of investments, or maybe your company only offers one choice of investment in your 401(k). Either way, while you are gainfully employed, your most impactful decision may just be the decision to continue funding your plan in the first place. But, when you are ready to retire or move jobs, you have choices to make requiring a little more thought and care.

When you are ready to part ways with your job, you have a few options:

- Leave the money where it is.
- Take the cash (and pay income taxes and perhaps a 10 percent additional federal tax if you are younger than age fifty-nine-and-one-half).
- Transfer the money to another employer plan (if the new plan allows).
- Roll the money over into a self-directed IRA.

Now, these are just general options. You will have to decide, hopefully with the help of a financial professional, what's right for you. For instance, 401(k)s are typically pretty closely tied to the companies offering them, so when changing jobs, it may not always be possible to transfer a 401(k) to another 401(k). Leaving the money where it is may also be out of the question—some companies have direct cash payout or rollover policies once someone is no longer employed.

Also, remember what we mentioned earlier about how we change jobs more often these days? That means you likely have a 401(k) with your current company, but you may also have a string of retirement accounts trailing you from other jobs.

When it comes to your retirement income, it's important to be able to pull together *all* your assets, so you can examine what you have and where, and then decide what you will do with it.

Tax-Qualified, Tax-Preferred, Tax-Deferred ... Still TAXED

Financial media often cite IRAs and 401(k)s for their tax benefits. After all, with traditional plans, you put your money in, pre-tax, and it hopefully grows for years, even decades, untaxed. That's why these accounts are called "tax-qualified" or "tax-deferred" assets. They aren't *tax-free!* Rarely does Uncle Sam allow business to continue without receiving his piece of the pie, and your retirement assets are no different. If you didn't pay taxes on the front end, you will pay taxes on the money you withdraw from these accounts in retirement.

Don't get me wrong: This isn't an inherently good or bad thing; it's just the way it is. It's important to understand, though, for the sake of planning ahead.

In retirement, many people assume they will be in a lower tax bracket. Are you planning to pare down your lifestyle in retirement? Perhaps you are, and perhaps you will have substantially less income in retirement. But many of my clients tell me they want to live life more or less the same as they always have. The money they would previously have spent on business attire or gas for their commute they now want to spend on hobbies and grandchildren. That's all fine, and for many of them, it is doable, but does it put them in a lower tax bracket? Probably not.

Keep in mind, IRAs, 401(k)s, and their alternatives have a few limitations because of their special tax status. For one thing, the IRS sets limits on your contributions to these retirement accounts. If you are contributing to a 401(k) or an equivalent nonprofit or government plan, your annual contribution limit is $20,500 (as of 2022). If you are fifty or older, the IRS allows additional contributions, called "catch-up contributions," of up to $6,500 on top of the regular limit of $20,500.[45] For an IRA, the limit is $7,000, with a catch-up limit of an additional $1,000.[46]

Because their tax advantages come from their intended use as retirement income, withdrawing funds from these accounts before you turn fifty-nine-and-one-half can carry stiff penalties. In addition to fees your investment management company might charge, you will have to pay income tax *and* a 10 percent federal tax penalty, with few exceptions.

The fifty-nine-and-one-half rule for retirement accounts is incredibly important to remember, especially when you're young. Younger workers are often tempted to cash out an IRA from a previous employer and then are surprised to find their checks missing

---

[45] Jackie Stewart. Kiplinger.com. Dec. 17, 2021. "401(k) Contribution Limits for 2022." https://www.kiplinger.com/retirement/retirement-plans/401ks/603949/401k-contribution-limits-for-2022
[46] Fidelity.com. 2021. "IRA contribution limits." https://www.fidelity.com/retirement-ira/contribution-limits-deadlines

20 percent of the account value to income taxes, penalty taxes, and account fees.

This poses a potential dilemma for millennials. While they may be socking money away in their workplace retirement plan, it is often the *only* place they are saving. This could be problematic later because of the fifty-nine-and-one-half rule; what if you have an emergency? It is important to fund your retirement, but you need to have some liquid assets handy as emergency funds. This can help you avoid breaking into your retirement accounts and incurring taxes and penalties because of the fifty-nine-and-one-half rule.

RMDs

Remember how we talked about the 401(k) or IRA being a "tax wrapper" for your funds? Well, eventually, Uncle Sam will want a bite of that candy bar. So, when you turn seventy-three, the government requires you withdraw a portion of your account, which the IRS calculates based on the size of your account and your estimated lifespan. This required minimum distribution, or RMD, is the government's insurance it will collect some taxes, at some point, from your earnings. Because you didn't pay taxes on the front end, you will now pay income taxes on whatever you withdraw, including your RMDs. Also, let me just remind you not to play chicken with the U.S. government; if you don't take your RMDs starting at seventy-three, you will have to write a check to the IRS for *50 percent* of the amount of your missed RMDs. With the change in law from the SECURE Act of 2019, followed by the SECURE 2.0 Act of 2022, even after you begin RMDs, you can still also continue contributing to your 401(k) or IRAs if you are still employed, which can affect the whole discussion on RMDs and possible tax considerations.

If you don't need income from your retirement accounts, RMDs can seem like more of a tax burden than an income boon. While some people prefer to reinvest their RMDs, this comes with the possibility of additional taxation: You'll pay income taxes on your RMDs and then capital gains taxes on the growth of your investments. If you are legacy-minded, there are other ways to use RMDs, many of which have tax benefits.

Permanent Life Insurance

One way to turn those pesky RMDs into a legacy is through permanent life insurance. Assuming you need the death benefit coverage and can qualify for it medically, if properly structured, these products can pass on a sizeable death benefit to your beneficiaries, tax-free, as part of your general legacy plan.

ILIT

Another way to use RMDs toward your legacy is to work with an estate planning attorney to create an irrevocable life insurance trust (ILIT). This is basically a permanent life insurance policy placed within a trust. Because the trust is irrevocable, you would relinquish control of it, but, unlike with just a permanent life insurance policy, your death benefit won't count toward your taxable estate.

Annuities

Because annuities can be tax-deferred, using all or a portion of your RMDs to fund an annuity contract can be one way to further delay taxation while guaranteeing your income payments (either to you or your loved ones) later. (Assuming you don't need the RMD income during your retirement.)

Qualified Charitable Distributions

If you are charity-minded, you may use your RMDs toward a charitable organization instead of using them for income. You must do this directly from your retirement account (you can't take the RMD check and *then* pay the charity) for your withdrawals to be qualified charitable distributions (QCDs), but this is one way of realizing some of the benefits of a charitable legacy during your own lifetime. You will not need to pay taxes on your QCDs, and they won't count toward your annual charitable tax deduction limit, plus you'll be able to see how the organization you are supporting uses your donations. You should consult a financial professional on how to correctly make a QCD, particularly since the SECURE Act has implemented a few regulations on this point.[47]

Roth IRA

Since the Taxpayer Relief Act of 1997, there has been a different kind of retirement account, or "tax wrapper," available to the public: the Roth. Roth IRAs and Roth 401(k)s differ from their traditional counterparts in one big way: You pay your taxes on the front end. This means, once your post-tax money is in the Roth account, as long as you follow the rules and limitations of that account, your distributions are truly tax-free. You won't pay income tax when you take withdrawals, so, in turn, you don't have to worry about RMDs. However, Roth accounts have the same limitations as traditional 401(k)s and IRAs when it comes to withdrawing money before age fifty-nine-and-one-half, with the added stipulation that the account must have been open for at least five years in order for the account holder to make withdrawals.

Taking Charge

As mentioned earlier, the 401(k) and IRA have largely replaced pensions, but they aren't an equal trade.

Pensions are employer-funded; the money feeding into them is money that wouldn't ever show up on your pay stub. Because 401(k)s are self-funded, you must actively and consciously save. This distinction has made a difference when it comes to funding retirement. The average 401(k) balance for a person aged sixty to sixty-nine is $195,500, but the median likely tells the full story. The median 401(k) balance for a person aged sixty to sixty-nine is $62,000. A general suggestion derived from those statistics is to aim, by age

---

47 Bob Carlson. Forbes. January 28, 2020. "More Questions And Answers About The SECURE Act." https://www.forbes.com/sites/bobcarlson/2020/01/28/more-questions-and-answers-about-the-secure-act/#113d49564869

thirty, to have saved an amount equal to 50 to 100 percent of your annual salary.[48] For some thirty-year-olds, saving half an annual salary by age thirty is more than some sixty-to-sixty-nine-year-olds have saved for their entire lives.

There can be many reasons why people underfund their retirement plans, like being overwhelmed by the investment choices or taking withdrawals from IRAs when they leave an employer. Still, the reason at the top of the list is this: People simply aren't participating to begin with.

So, whether you use a 401(k) with an employer or an IRA alternative with a private company, separate from your workplace, the most important retirement savings decision you can make is to sock away your money somewhere in the first place.

---

[48] Arielle O'Shea. Nerd Wallet. March 17, 2021. "The Average 401(k) Balance by Age." https://www.nerdwallet.com/article/investing/the-average-401k-balance-by-age

CHAPTER 7

Annuities

In my practice, I offer my clients a variety of products—from securities to insurance—all designed to help them reach their financial goals. You may be wondering: Why single out a single product in this book?

Well, while most of my clients have a pretty good understanding of business and finance, I sometimes find those who have the impression there must be magic involved. Some people assume there is a magic finance wand we can wave to change years' worth of savings into a strategy for retirement income. But it's not as easy as a goose laying golden eggs or the Fairy Godmother turning a pumpkin into a coach!

Finances aren't magic; it takes lots of hard work and, typically, several financial products and strategies to pull together a complete retirement plan. Of all the financial products our advisors work with, it seems people find none more mysterious than annuities. And, if I may say, even some of those who recognize the word "annuity" have a limited understanding of the product. So, in the interest of demystifying annuities, let me tell you a little about what an annuity is.

The origins of annuities date back to ancient Rome. Contracts during the Emperor's time were known as *annua*, or "annual stipends" in Latin. Back then, Roman citizens would make a one-time payment to the *annua* in exchange for lifetime payments made once a year.

They also have a long history in America, dating back to the founding of the country. In 1759, a company in Pennsylvania was formed to benefit presbyterian ministers and their families. Ministers would contribute to the fund in exchange for lifetime payments.

It wasn't until 1912 that Americans could buy annuities outside of a group. The Pennsylvania Company for Insurance on Lives and Granting Annuities was the very first American company to offer annuities to the general public.

And did you know this? Ben Franklin used them. He actually left an annuity to the City of Boston that continued to pay right up to the 1990s (nearly 200 years later!), until the city decided to receive a lump-sum payment.

Annuities continue to be extraordinarily popular in modern times.

In general, insurance is a financial hedge against risk. Car owners buy auto insurance to protect their finances in case they injure someone, or someone injures them. Homeowners have house insurance to protect their finances in case of a fire, flood, or another disaster. People have life insurance to protect their finances in case of untimely death. Almost juxtaposed to life insurance, people have annuities in case of a long life; annuities can give you financial protection by providing consistent and reliable income payments.

The basic premise of an annuity is you, the annuitant, pay an insurance company some amount in exchange for their contractual guarantee they will pay you income for a certain time period. How that company pays you, for how long, and how much they offer are all determined by the annuity contract you enter into with the insurance company.

How You Get Paid

There are two ways for an annuity contract to provide income: The first is through what is called annuitization, and the second is through the use of income riders. We'll get into income riders in a bit, but let's talk about annuitization. That nice, long word is, in my opinion, one reason annuities have a reputation for mystery and misinformation.

Annuitization

When someone "annuitizes" a contract, it is the point where he or she turns on the income stream. Once a contract has been annuitized, there is no going back. With annuities, if the policyholder lives longer than the insurance company planned, the insurance company is still obligated to pay him or her, even if the payments end up being way more than the contract's actual value. If, however, the policyholder dies an untimely death, depending on the contract type, the insurance company may keep anything left of the money that funded the annuity—nothing would be paid out to the contract holder's survivors. You see where that could make some people balk? Now, modern annuities rarely rely on annuitization for the income portion of the contract, and instead have so many bells and whistles that the old concept of annuitization seems outdated, but because this is still an option, it's important to at least understand the basic concept.

Riders

Speaking of bells and whistles, let's talk about riders. Modern annuities have a lot of different options these days, many in the form of riders you can add to your contract for a fee—usually about 1 percent of the contract value per year. Each rider has its particulars, and the types of riders available will vary by the type of annuity contract purchased, but I'll just briefly outline some of these little extras:

- Lifetime income rider: Contract guarantees you an enhanced income for life
- Death benefit rider: Contract pays an enhanced death benefit to your beneficiaries even if you have annuitized
- Return of premium rider: Guarantees you (or your beneficiaries) will at least receive back the premium value of the annuity

- Long-term care rider: Provides a certain amount, sometimes as much as twice the principal value of the contract, to help pay for long-term care if the contract holder is moved to a nursing home or assisted living situation

This isn't an extensive look, and usually the riders have fancier names based on the issuing company, like "Lorem Ipsum Insurance Company Income Preferred Bonus Fixed Index Annuity rider," but I just wanted to show you what some of the general options are in layperson's terms.

Types of Annuities

Annuities break down into four basic types: immediate, variable, fixed, and fixed index.

Immediate

Immediate annuities primarily rely on annuitization to provide income—you give the insurance company a lump sum up front, and your payments begin immediately. Once you begin receiving income payments, the transaction is irreversible, and you no longer have access to your money in a lump sum. When you die, any remaining contract value is typically forfeited to the insurance company.

All other annuity contract types are "deferred" contracts, meaning you fund your policy as a lump sum or over a period of years and you give it the opportunity to grow over time—sometimes years, sometimes decades.

Variable

A variable annuity is an insurance contract, as well as an investment. It's sold by insurance companies, but only through someone who is registered to sell investment products. With a variable annuity contract, the insurance company invests your premiums in subaccounts that are tied to the stock market. This makes it a bit different from the other annuity contract types because it is the only contract where your money is subject to losses because of market declines. Your contract value has a greater opportunity to grow, but it also stands to lose. Additionally, your contract's value will be subject to the underlying investment's fees and limitations—including capital gains taxes, management fees, etc. Once it is time for you to receive income from the contract, the insurance company will pay you a certain income, locked in at whatever your contract's value was.

Fixed

A traditional fixed annuity is pretty straightforward. You purchase a contract with a guaranteed interest rate and, when you are ready, the insurance company will make regular income payments to you at whatever payout rate your contract guarantees. Those payments will continue for the rest of your life and, if you choose, for the remainder of your spouse's life.

Fixed annuities don't have much in the way of upside potential, but many people like them for their guarantees (after all, if your Aunt May lives to be ninety-five, knowing she has a paycheck later in life can be her mental and financial safety net), as well as for their predictability. Unlike variable annuities, which are subject to market risk and might be up one year and down the next, you can easily calculate the value of your fixed annuity over your lifetime.

Fixed Index

To recap, variable annuities take on more risk to offer more possibilities to grow. Fixed annuities have less potential growth, but they protect your principal. In the last couple of decades, many insurance companies have retooled their product line to offer fixed index annuities, which are sort of midway between variable and fixed annuities on that risk/reward spectrum. Fixed index annuities offer greater growth potential than traditional fixed annuities but less than variable annuities. Like traditional fixed annuities, however, fixed index annuities are protected from downside market losses.

Fixed index annuities earn interest that is tied to the market, meaning that, instead of your contract value growing at a set interest rate like a traditional fixed annuity, it has the potential to grow within a range. Your contract's value is credited interest based on the performance of an external market index like the S&P 500 while never being invested in the market itself. You can't invest in the S&P 500 directly, but each year, your annuity as the potential to earn interest based on the chosen index's performance, submit to limits set by the company such as caps, spreads and participation rates. For instance, if your contract caps your interest at 5 percent, then in a year that the S&P 500 gains 3 percent, your annuity value increases 3 percent. If the S&P 500 gains 35 percent, your annuity value gets a 5 percent interest bump. But since your money isn't actually invested in the market with a fixed index annuity, if the market nosedives (such as happened during 2000, 2008, and 2020, anyone?) you won't see any increase in your contract value. Conversely, there will also be no decrease in your contract value—no matter how badly the market performed, as long as you follow the terms of the contract, you won't lose any of the interest you were credited in previous years.

So, what if the S&P 500 shows a market loss of 30 percent? Your contract value isn't going anywhere (unless you purchased an optional rider—this charge will still come out of your annuity value each year). For those who are more interested in protection than growth potential, fixed index annuities can be an attractive option because, when the stock market has a long period of positive performance, a fixed index annuity can enjoy conservative growth. And, during stretches where the stock market is erratic and stock values across the board take significant losses? Fixed index annuities won't lose anything due to the stock market volatility.

Our experience shows that annuities get extra attention during periods of market turmoil. If you go back to the financial crisis that spawned "The Great Recession," in 2008-2009 and in its aftermath, there was renewed interest in annuities as a means to manage risk. And if we look back over 2022, annuities gained favor with many of our clients as they assessed greater volatility and higher inflation. Not to mention a rising interest rate environment.

Other Things to Know About Annuities

We just talked about the four kinds of annuity contracts available, but all of them have some commonalities as annuities.

For all annuities, the contractual guarantees are only as strong as the insurance company that sells the product, which makes it important to thoroughly check the credit ratings of any company whose products you are considering.

Annuities are tax-deferred, meaning you don't have to pay taxes on interest earnings each year as the contract value grows. Instead, you will pay ordinary income taxes on your withdrawals. These are meant to be long-term products, so, like other tax-deferred or tax-advantaged products, if you begin taking withdrawals from your contract before age fifty-nine-and-one-half, you may also have to pay a 10 percent federal tax penalty. Also, while annuities are generally considered illiquid, most contracts allow you to withdraw up to 10 percent of your contract value every year. Withdraw any more, however, and you could incur additional surrender penalties.

Keep in mind, your withdrawals will deplete the accumulated cash value, death benefit, and, possibly, the rider values of your contract.

Make no mistake about it, annuities are a polarizing product. We tend to find people who either love annuities or hate them; their emotions run the gambit from being the best decision they've ever made in entering into an annuity contract to the worst decision they have ever made.

Each camp has good reason behind their personal experience with annuities. For some, the fees associated with them are deemed exorbitant, the riders appear terribly complex, and they get confused on the surrender time periods. On the other hand, people like the steady income stream the product provides, riders can provide a unique opportunity to customize individual needs, and they can offer tax advantages.

On a fundamental level, annuities are really risk management products. It may be useful to view annuities from this perspective: Assess your own risks. Does it make sense to shift some risk off your personal balance sheet and place it on the balance sheet of an insurance company, even with the costs associated with working with that company, or not?

Annuities aren't for everyone, but it's important to understand them before saying "yea" or "nay" on whether they fit into your plan; otherwise, you're not operating with complete information, wouldn't you agree? Regardless, you should talk to a financial professional who can help you understand annuities, help you dissect your particular financial needs, and help show you whether an annuity is appropriate for your retirement income plan. That professional also can help you weigh the risk/reward quotient and see if an annuity is right for you.

CHAPTER 8

Estate & Legacy

I n my practice, we devote a significant portion of our time to matters of estates. That doesn't mean drawing up wills or trusts or putting together powers of attorney or anything like that. After all, I'm not an estate planning attorney. But I am a financial professional, and what part of the "estate" isn't affected by money matters?

I've included this chapter because we have seen many people do estate planning wrong. Clients, or clients' families, have come in after experiencing a death in the family and have found themselves in the middle of probate, high taxes, or a discovery of something unforeseen (often long-term care) draining the estate.

We also have seen people do estate planning right: clients or families who visit my office to talk about legacies and how to make them last and adult children who have room to grieve without an added burden of unintended costs, without stress from a family ruptured because of inadequate planning.

I'll share some of these stories here. However, I'm not going to give you specific advice, since everyone's situation is unique. I only want to give you some things to think about and to underscore the importance of planning ahead.

As I mentioned earlier, we are not tax professionals at Kelly Financial. And it is important to underscore here that we are not estate and legacy professionals. We have a solid working knowledge of estate planning. However, we do work closely with a number of strategic partners who are in fact experts in this field. And our clients have been the beneficiaries of these relationships. Some clients bring with them their own estate and legacy attorneys while others need such referrals. The key to these relationships is obvious—not only working with reputable people but people who communicate well between and with client and financial professional, and understand the financial impacts of their advice along with the aspirations of our clients.

You Can't Take It With You

When it comes to legacy and estate planning, the most important thing is to *do it*. I have heard people from clients to celebrities (rap artist Snoop Dogg comes to mind) say they aren't interested in what happens to their assets when they die because they'll be dead. That's certainly one way to look at it. But I think that's a very selfish way to go about things—we all have people and causes we care about, and those who care about us. Even if the people we love don't *need* what we leave behind, they still can be fined or legally tied up in the probate process or burial costs if we don't plan for those. And that's not even considering what happens if you become incapacitated at some point while you are still alive. Having a plan in place can greatly reduce the stress of those responsibilities on your loved ones; it's just a loving thing to do.

Documents

There are a few documents that lay the groundwork of legacy planning. You've probably heard of all or most of them, but I'd like to review what they are and how people commonly use them. These are all things you should talk about with an estate planning attorney to establish your legacy.

Powers of Attorney

A power of attorney, or POA, is a document giving someone the authority to act on your behalf and in your best interests. These come in handy in situations where you cannot be present (think a vacation where you get stuck in Canada) or, for durable powers of attorney, even when you are incapacitated (think in a coma or coping with dementia).

It is important to have powers of attorney in place and to appoint someone you trust to act on your behalf in these matters. Have you ever heard of someone who was incapacitated after a car accident, whether from head trauma or being in a coma for weeks—sometimes months? Do you think their bills stopped coming due during that time? I like my phone company and my bank, but neither one is about to put a moratorium on sending me bills, particularly not for an extended or interminable period. A power of attorney would have the authority to pay your mortgage or cancel your cable while you are unable.

You can have multiple POAs and require them to act jointly.

What this looks like: Do you think two heads are better than one? One man, Chris, significantly relied on his two sons' opinions for both his business and personal matters. He appointed both sons as joint POA, requiring both their signoffs for his medical and financial matters.

You can have multiple POAs who can act independently.

What this looks like: Irene had three children with whom she routinely stayed. They lived in different areas of the country, which she thought was an advantage; one month she might be hiking out West, the next she could enjoy the newest off-Broadway production, and the next she could soak up some Southern sun. She named her three children as independently authorized POAs, so, if something happened, no matter where she was, the child closest could step in to act on her behalf.

You can have POAs who have different responsibilities.

What this looks like: Although Luke's friend Claire, a nurse, was his go-to and POA for health-related issues, financial matters usually made her nervous, so he appointed his good neighbor, Matt, as his POA in all of his financial and legal matters.

In addition to POAs, it may be helpful to have an advanced medical directive. This is a document where you have pre-decided what choices you would make about different health scenarios. An advanced medical directive can help ease the burden for your medical POA and loved ones, particularly when it comes to end-of-life care.

Wills

Perhaps the most basic document of legacy planning, a will is a legal document wherein you outline your wishes for your estate. When it comes to your estate after your death, having a will is the foundation of your legacy. Without one, your loved ones are left behind, guessing what you would have wanted, and the court likely will split your assets according to the state's defaults. Maybe that's exactly what you wanted, as far as anyone knows, right? Because even if you told your nephew he could have your car he's been driving, if it's not in writing, it still might go to the brother, sister, son, or daughter to whom you aren't speaking.

However, it may not be enough just to have a will. Even with a will, your assets will be subject to probate. Probate is what we call the state's process for determining a will's validity. A judge will go through your will to question if it conflicts with state law, if it is the most up-to-date document, if you were mentally competent at the time it was in order, etc. For some, this is a quick, easily-resolved process. For others, particularly if someone steps forward to contest the will, it may take years to settle, all the while subjecting the assets to court costs and attorney's fees.

One other undesirable piece of the probate process is that it is a public process. That means anyone can go to the courthouse, ask for copies of the case, and discover your assets. They can also see who is slated to receive what and who is disputing.

It's also important to remember beneficiary lines trump wills. So, that large life insurance policy? What if, when you bought it fifteen years ago, you wrote your ex-husband's name on the beneficiary line? Even if you stipulate otherwise in your will, the company that holds your policy will pay out to your ex-spouse. Or, how about the thousands of dollars in your IRA you dedicated to the children thirty years ago, but one of your children was killed in a car accident, leaving his wife and two toddlers behind? That IRA is going to transfer to your remaining children, with nothing for your daughter-in-law and grandchildren.

That may paint a grim portrait, but I can't underscore enough the importance of working with a skilled estate planning attorney to keep your will and beneficiary lines up to date as your life changes.

Many people are under the impression that estate and legacy planning is only for the uber rich and famous. But let me dispel that notion. Many of the pages you are reading focus on the generation and preservation of wealth. But if you have good intentions for the distribution of your wealth, you will want to consider working with an estate and legacy professional.

And just think of some rich and famous rock stars who reportedly did not have a will or trust: Aretha Franklin, Prince, and Sonny Bono come to mind. So, avoid the costly, and sometimes disputacious, painful process of probate.

Trusts

Another piece of legacy planning to consider is the trust. A trust is set up through an attorney and allows a third party, or trustee, to hold your assets and determine how they will pass to your beneficiaries.

Many people are skeptical of trusts because they assume trusts are only appropriate for the fabulously wealthy.

However, a simple trust will likely cost more than $1,000 if prepared by an attorney and fees can be higher for couples.[49] But a trust can help you avoid both the expense and publicity of probate, provide a more immediate transfer of wealth, avoid some taxes, and provide you greater control over your legacy.

For instance, if you want to set aside some funds for a grandchild's college education, you can make it a requirement he or she enrolls in classes before your trust will dispense any funds. Like a will, beneficiary lines will override your trust conditions, so you must keep insurance policies and other assets up to date.

Like any financial or legal consideration, there are many options these days beyond the simple "yes or no" question of whether to have a trust. For one thing, you will need to consider if you want your trust to be revocable (you can change the terms while you are alive) or irrevocable (can't be changed; you are no longer the "owner" of the contents). A brief note here about irrevocable trusts: Although they have significant and greater tax benefits, they are still subject to a Medicaid look-back period. This means, if you transfer your assets into an irrevocable trust in an attempt to shelter them from a Medicaid spend-down, you will be ineligible for Medicaid coverage of long-term care for five years. Yet, an irrevocable trust can avoid both probate and estate taxes, and it can even protect assets from legal judgments against you.

Another thing to remember when it comes to trusts, in general, is, even if you have set up a trust, you must remember to fund it. In my two decades of work, we've had numerous clients come to us, assuming they have protected their assets with a trust. When we talk about taxes and other pieces of their legacy, it turns out they never retitled any assets or changed any paperwork on the assets they wanted in the trust. So, please remember, a trust is just a bunch of

---

[49] Rickie Houston. smartasset.com. "How Much Does It Cost to Set Up a Trust?" https://smartasset.com/estate-planning/how-much-does-it-cost-to-set-up-a-trust

fancy legal papers if you haven't followed through on retitling your assets.

Taxes

Although charitable contributions, trusts, and other tax-efficient strategies can reduce your tax bill, it's unlikely your estate will be passed on entirely tax-free. Yet, when it comes to building a legacy that can last for generations, taxes can be one of the heaviest drains on the impact of your hard work.

For 2020, the federal estate exemption was $11.58 million per individual and $23.16 million for a married couple, with estates facing up to a 40 percent tax rate after that. In 2022, those limits increased to $12.06 million for individuals and $24.12 million for married couples, with the 40 percent top level gift and estate tax remaining the same. Currently, the new estate limits are set to increase with inflation until January 1, 2026, when they will "sunset" back to the inflation-adjusted 2017 limits.[50] And that's not taking into account the various state regulations and taxes regarding estate and inheritance transfers.

Another tax concern "frequent flyer": retirement accounts.

Your IRA or 401(k) can be a source of tax issues when you pass away. For one thing, taking funds from a sizeable account can trigger a large tax bill. However, if you leave the assets in the account, there are still required minimum distributions (RMDs), which will take effect even after you die. If you pass the account to your spouse, he or she can keep taking your RMDs as is, or your spouse can retitle the account in his or her name and receive RMDs based on his or her life expectancy. Remember, if you don't take your RMDs, the IRS will take up to 50 percent of whatever your required distribution was, plus you will still have to pay income taxes whenever you withdraw

---

[50] Laura Sanders, Richard Rubin. The Wall Street Journal. March 10, 2022. "Estate and Gift Taxes 2021-2022: "What's New This Year and What You Need to Know." https://www.wsj.com/articles/estate-and-gift-taxes-what-to-know-2021-2022-11646426764

that money. Thanks to the enactment of the SECURE Act, anyone who inherits your IRA, with few exceptions (your spouse, a beneficiary less than ten years younger, or a disabled adult child, to name a few), will need to empty the account within ten years of your death.[51]

Also—and this is a pretty big also—check with an attorney if you are considering putting your IRA or 401(k) in a trust. An improperly titled beneficiary form for the IRA could mean the difference of thousands of dollars in taxes. This is just one more reason to work with a financial professional, one who can strategically partner with an estate planning attorney to diligently check your decisions.

*****

Before we leave the topic of estate and legacy, here are some final thoughts.

We like to be the main focal point of any financial related matter for our clients' retirement concerns. And when it comes to estate planning, while we do not formulate the intricacies of an entire estate plan, we do enact it. And here is something to give serious consideration to. The advisors at Kelly Financial Services have seen many situations where people have paid thousands of dollars to set up the most in-depth estate plan but never implemented it. Imagine that!

It is easy to understand that the first step is getting all the documentation together and fully executed. But then it is up to the client and their financial professionals to start to implement it.

The implementation of a plan is imperative. It includes updating the beneficiaries of the accounts and retitling certain accounts into a trust. Another important part of an estate plan is the real estate. In some cases, the house needs to be put into a trust; this is a process the estate planner should assist with. But it is the one part that we see overlooked the most.

Finally, the plan needs to be reviewed every three to five years. Much goes into establishing the plan and over time things change.

---

[51] Julia Kagan. Investopedia. October 11, 2020. "Stretch IRA." https://www.investopedia.com/terms/s/stretch-ira.asp

Beneficiaries might need to be updated, assets values might need revision, and most importantly rules and regulations might change.

Reviewing any trust and legacy plan can be made part of the larger review process of the financial professional.

CHAPTER 9

Women Retire Too

I help men, women, and families from all walks of life on their journey to and through retirement. Yet, I want to address the female demographic specifically. Why?

This topic was always important to me, but it really hit home after Bill passed. In a flash, on that fateful day in October 2017, I became a widow, a single mom, a CEO, and a client of the firm. I always thought I would go before Bill, despite the fact that he was older by a number of years. Nevertheless, we prepared for the possibility from a financial standpoint, as best we could. But speaking from my experience, you are never fully prepared—especially emotionally—when a loved one passes. I believe this is so whether it happens suddenly or expectedly.

There are many important lessons here that I hope you will take heart and take note. I cannot stress enough how critical it is to have a plan in place for when the inevitable happens. This might be the most important chapter in the book.

The topics, products, and strategies I cover elsewhere in this book are meant to help address retirement concerns for men *and* women, but much of traditional planning is geared toward men. Male careers, male lifespans, male health care. The bottom line is women's career paths often look much different than men's, so why would their retirement planning look the same?

Women often embrace different roles and values than men as workers, wives, mothers, and daughters. They are more apt to take on roles as caretakers. They often plan for events, worry about loved ones, tend to details, and think about the future. Also, they often want everything to be just right, and they want to be right themselves. It could be you've seen the following affixed to a decorative sign, refrigerator magnet, or T-shirt: "If I agreed with you, we'd both be wrong." The barb features a picture of a woman speaking to a man.

If these characteristics I listed about women are accurate, shouldn't they deserve special considerations from financial professionals? The case can be made, particularly since 70 percent of men in the U.S. age sixty-five and older happen to be married, compared to 48 percent of women in that age classification.[52] Single women don't have the opportunity to capitalize on the resource pooling and economies of scale accompanying a marriage or partnership.

In another sad development, women are more likely to deal with poverty than men when they reach retirement. In 2020, the overall poverty rate for women (16.4 percent) exceeded the rate for men (15.7 percent).[53]

Speaking of relevant statistics, here is one that still blows my mind. According to the Women's Institute for a Secure Retirement, 80 percent of men die married but 80 percent of women die single.

So while much of the arithmetic and concepts in this book are the same regardless of gender or marital status, retirement planning for women needs to be different because of these special challenges that are unique to them. I know this firsthand.

Yes, this chapter is for women, it is also important for anyone who has a woman in their lives that they care about.

---

[52] Administration for Community Living. May 27, 2021. "Profile of Older Americans." https://acl.gov/aging-and-disability-in-america/data-and-research/profile-older-americans

[53] statistica.com. 2022. "Poverty rate in the United States in 2020, by age and gender." https://www.statista.com/statistics/233154/us-poverty-rate-by-gender/

Be Informed

It's a familiar scene in many financial offices across the country: A woman comes into an appointment carrying a sack full of unopened envelopes. Often through tears, she sits across the desk from a financial professional and apologizes her way through a conversation about what financial products she owns and where her income is coming from. She is recently widowed and was sure her spouse was taking care of the finances, but now she doesn't know where all their assets are kept, and her confidence in her financial outlook has wavered after walking through funeral expenses and realizing she's down to one income.

Often, she may be financially "okay." Yet, the uncertainty can be wearying, particularly when the family is already reeling from a loss. While this scenario sometimes plays out with men, in my experience, it's more likely to be a woman in that chair across from my desk, probably, in part, because of Western traditions about money management being "a guy thing." But it doesn't have to be this way. This all-too-common scenario can be wiped away with just a little preparation.

Talk to Your Spouse/ Work with a Financial Professional

While there are many factors affecting women's financial preparation for and situation in retirement, I cannot emphasize enough that the decision to be informed, to be a part of the conversation, and to be aware of what is going on with your finances is absolutely paramount to a confident retirement. With all the couples I've seen, there is almost always an "alpha" when it comes to finances. It isn't always men—for many of my coupled clients, the wife is the alpha who keeps the books and budgets and knows where all of the family's assets are, down to the penny—yet, statistically, among baby boomers it is usually a man who runs the books. But, as time goes on, it looks like the ratio of male to female financial alphas is evening out.

According to a 2019 Gallup study, women are equally as likely to take the lead on finances as men, with 37 percent of U.S. households showing women primarily paying the bills. Half of households also say decisions about savings and investments are shared equally.[54] Whether that's the way your household works or not, there isn't anything wrong with who does what.

The breakdown happens when there is a lack of communication, when no one other than the financial alpha knows how much the family has and where. In the end, it doesn't matter who handles the money; it's about all parties being informed of what's going on financially.

There are a lot of ways to open the conversation about money. One woman started a conversation with her husband, the financial alpha, by sitting down and saying, "Teach me how to be a widow." Perhaps that sounds grim, but it was to the point, and it spurred what she said was a very fruitful conversation.

They spent a day, just one part of an otherwise dull weekend, going through everything she might need to know. They spent the better part of two decades together after that. When he died, and she was widowed, she said the "widowhood" talk had made a huge difference. She knew who to call to talk through their retirement plan and where to call for the insurance policy.

Years later, she accompanied a recently widowed friend of hers to a financial appointment. Her friend was emotional the whole time, afraid she would run out of money any day. The financial professional ultimately showed the friend that she was financially in good shape, but not before the friend had already spent months worried that each check would exhaust her bank account. That's no way to live after losing a loved one. It was preventable had her deceased spouse and financial professional included her in a conversation about "widowhood."

---

[54] Megan Brenan. Gallup. January 29, 2020. "Women Still Handle Main Household Tasks in U.S." https://news.gallup.com/poll/283979/women-handle-main-household-tasks.aspx

Couples sometimes have their first real conversation about money, assets, and their retirement income approach, in our office. The important thing about having these conversations isn't where, it's when... and the best "when" is as soon as possible.

And here's another thing. Every financial professional who works with couples should understand this reality: When a couple leaves the office after that first meeting, they will head back to their car, thoughts racing with all the financial and planning information they just discussed and contemplated. Inevitably, the husband will look at his wife. Depending on his confidence level—sheepishly, optimistically, or bravely—he will ask, "So what did you think?"

Her response, and the attendant tone carried with it, will dictate whether or not the couple proceeds with working with the financial professional. It is a delicate balance for the financial professional. The needs of the couple must also include the needs of the wife. Conceptually, it is easy to understand. But in reality, it is a challenge to execute a plan to meet the needs for both. It must be separate but equal.

Spouse-Specific Options

One area where it might be especially important to be on the same page between spouses is when it comes to financial products or services that have spousal options. A few that come to mind are pensions and Social Security, although life insurance and annuity policies also have the potential to affect both spouses.

With pensions, taking the worker's life-only option is somewhat attractive—after all, the monthly payment is bigger. However, you and your spouse should discuss your options. When we're talking about both of you, as opposed to just one lifespan, there is an increased likelihood at least one of you will live a long, long time. This means the monthly payout will be less, but it also ensures that, no matter which spouse outlives the other, no one will have to suffer the loss of a needed pension paycheck in his or her later retirement years.

While we covered Social Security options in a different chapter, I think some of the spousal information bears repeating. Particularly, if you worked exclusively inside the home for a significant number of years, you may want to talk about taking your Social Security benefits based on your spouse's work history. After all, Social Security is based on your thirty-five highest-earning years.

Things to remember about the spousal benefits:[55]

- Your benefit will be calculated as a percentage (up to 50 percent) of your spouse's earned monthly benefit at his or her full retirement age, or FRA.

- For you to begin receiving a spousal benefit, your spouse must have already filed for his or her own benefits and you must be at least sixty-two.

- You can qualify for a full half of your spouse's benefits if you wait until you reach FRA to file.

- Beginning your benefits earlier than your FRA will reduce your monthly check but waiting to file until after FRA will not increase your benefits.

For divorcees:[56]

- You may qualify for an ex-spousal benefit if . . .
    a. You were married for a decade or more
    b. *and* you are at least sixty-two
    c. *and* you have been divorced for at least two years
    d. *and* you are currently unmarried
    e. *and* your ex-spouse is sixty-two (qualifies to begin taking Social Security)

- Your ex-spouse does not need to have filed for you to file on his or her benefit.

- Similar to spousal benefits, you can qualify for up to half of your ex-spouse's benefits if you wait to file until your FRA.

---

[55] Social Security Administration. "Retirement Planner: Benefits For You As A Spouse." https://www.ssa.gov/planners/retire/applying6.html
[56] Social Security Administration. "Retirement Planner: If You Are Divorced." https://www.ssa.gov/planners/retire/divspouse.html

- If your ex-spouse dies, you may file to receive a widow/widower benefit on his or her Social Security record as long as you are at least age sixty and fulfill all the other requirements on the preceding alphabetized list.
  a. This will not affect the benefits of your ex-spouse's current spouse

For widow's (or widower's, for that matter) benefits:[57]
- You may qualify to receive as much as your deceased spouse would have received if...
  a. You were married for at least nine months before his or her death
  b. *or* you would qualify for a divorced spousal benefit
  c. *and* you are at least sixty
  d. *and* you did not/have not remarried before age sixty
- You may earn delayed credits on your spouse's benefit *if* your spouse hadn't already filed for benefits when he or she died.
- Other rules may apply to you if you are disabled or are caring for a deceased spouse's dependent or disabled child.

Longevity

On average, women live longer than men. Most stats put average female longevity at about two years more than men. But averages are tricky things. An April 2022 report by the World Economic Forum listed the eight oldest people in the world to all be women. They ranged in age from 118 years old to 114 and included two Americans.[58]

On one hand, this is a Brandi Chastain moment. You know, when the American soccer icon shed her jersey to celebrate a game-winning

[57] Social Security Administration. "Survivors Planner: If You Are The Worker's Widow Or Widower." https://www.ssa.gov/planners/survivors/ifyou.html#h2
[58] Martin Armstrong. World Economic Forum. April 29, 2022. "How old are the world's oldest people?" https://www.weforum.org/agenda/2022/04/the-oldest-people-in-the-world/

penalty kick to win the World Cup. Seriously, how fabulous are women? They tend to be meticulous, resolute, perseverant. On the other hand, the trend for women to live longer presents longstanding financial ramifications.

Simply Needing More Money in Retirement

Living longer in retirement means needing more money, period. Barring a huge lottery win or some crazy stock market action, the date you retire is likely the point at which you have the most money you will ever have. Not to put too grim a spin on it, but the problem with longevity is, the further you get away from that date, the further your dollars have to stretch. If you planned to live to a nice eighty-something but live to a nice one-hundred-something, that is *two decades* you will need to account for, monetarily.

To put this in perspective, let's say you like to drink coffee as an everyday splurge. Not accounting for inflation or leap years, a $2.50 cup-a-day habit is $18,250 over a two-decade span. Now, think of all the things you like to do that cost money. Add those up for twenty years of unanticipated costs. I think you'll see what I mean.

During the 2020 onset of the coronavirus pandemic, many learned to cut costs. For some, that amounted to skipping their decadent latte. For others, however, cutbacks became acute. According to data compiled by Age Wave and Edward Jones, 32 percent of Americans plan to retire later than planned because of the pandemic. Women felt a more adverse effect. The report stipulated that 41 percent of women continued to save for retirement, compared to 58 percent of men.[59]

---

[59] Megan Leonhardt. cnbc.com. June 16, 2021. "58% of men were able to continue saving for retirement during the pandemic—but only 41% of women were." https://www.cnbc.com/2021/06/16/why-pandemic-hit-womens-retirement-savings-more-than-mens.html

More Health Care Needs

In addition to the cost of living for a longer lifespan is the fact aging, plain and simple, means more health care, and more health care means more money. Women are survivors. They suffer from the morbidity-mortality paradox, which states women suffer more non-fatal illnesses throughout their lifetime than men, who experience fewer illnesses but higher mortality.

Women have been found to seek treatment more often when not feeling well and emphasize staying healthy when older, according to studies.[60] So survival is on the side of the woman. However, surviving things, like cancer, also means more checkups later in life.

Widowhood

Not only do women typically live longer than their same-age male counterparts, they also have the tendency to marry men older than themselves. The numbers bear this out: Worldwide, one in five women live in a solo household after turning sixty compared to one in ten men.[61]

I don't write this to scare people; rather, I think it's fundamentally important to prepare my female clients for something that may be a startling, *but very likely,* scenario. At some point, most women will have to handle their financial situations on their own. A little preparation can go a long way and having a basic understanding of your household finances and the "who, what, where, and how much" of your family's assets is incredibly useful—it can prevent a tragic situation from being more traumatic.

In my opinion, the financial services industry sometimes underserves women in these situations. Some financial professionals

---

[60] advisory.com. July 22, 2020. "Why do women live longer than men? It's more complicated than you think." https://www.advisory.com/en/daily-briefing/2020/07/22/longevity

[61] Jacob Ausubel. Pew Research Center. January 3, 2020. "Globally, women are younger than their male partners, more likely to age alone." https://www.pewresearch.org/fact-tank/2020/01/03/globally-women-are-younger-than-their-male-partners-more-likely-to-age-alone/

tend to alienate women, even when their spouses are alive. I've heard several stories of women who sat through meeting after meeting without their financial professional ever addressing a single question to them.

In our firm, when we work with couples, we work hard to make sure our retirement income strategies work for *both* people. No matter who the financial alpha is, it's important for everyone affected by a retirement strategy to understand it.

Taxes

One of the often-unexpected aspects of widowhood is the tax bill. Many women continue similar lifestyles to the ones they shared with their spouses. This, in turn, means continuing to have a similar need for income. However, after the death of a spouse, their taxes will be calculated based on a single filer's income table, which is much less forgiving than the couple's tax rates. With proper planning, your financial professional and tax advisor may be able to help you take the sting out of your new tax status.

Gray Divorce

I've been looking at a number of trends affecting retirees and pre-retirees these days, and one really caught my attention—call it silver splitters, diamond divorcees, or gray divorce.

Traditionally, older couples tended to stay married whether or not they felt satisfied and fulfilled. Unfortunately, this has changed rather dramatically.

While the U.S. divorce rate among younger couples has steadily declined, it is increasing dramatically with adults aged fifty and over. Are you ready for this? Since 1990, divorce rates have doubled for those fifty-plus, and they have tripled among those sixty-five and up.

Considering that couples in these age groups have spent many years together, and often have adult children and even grandchildren, the consequences of divorce may have an even greater impact on retirement finances.

For those of you who might find yourself involved in these unfortunate circumstances, while your retirement plans may shift due to divorce, it is possible to get through a divorce without having to start over.

I was contemplating if I should even mention this topic in these pages. Then again, because it is a growing problem, with so many new complexities to add to an abundance of complexities to begin with, after I decided to include it, the question was, where do I put it? Ultimately, I wanted to include it in this chapter because it presents special circumstances for women.

This problem doesn't look like it is going away. I wish the trends would reverse and I hope they do. All the same, it needs more attention from all parties involved.

Caregiving

Of the 53 million caregivers providing unpaid, informal care for older adults in 2020, 61 percent are women. Among today's family caregivers, 61 percent work and 45 percent report some kind of financial impact from providing a loved one care and support.[62] In addition to the financial burden created by caregiving responsibilities, women devote an average of 5.7 hours each day to duties such as housekeeping and looking after loved ones.[63] So then, when can women find the time to focus long and hard on financial matters?

Unfortunately, the impact and hardships created by traditional roles for women typically do not account for Social Security benefit losses or the losses of health care benefits and retirement savings. This also doesn't account for maternity care, mothers who

---

[62] caregiving.org. 2020 Report. "Caregiving in the U.S. 2020." https://www.caregiving.org/caregiving-in-the-us-2020/

[63] Drew Weisholtz. Today. January 22, 2020. "Women do 2 more hours of housework daily than men, study says." https://www.today.com/news/women-do-2-more-hours-housework-daily-men-study-says-t172272

homeschool, or women who leave the workforce to care for their children in any way.

I don't repeat these statistics to scare you. Estimates typically place the monetary value of unofficial caregiving services across the United States at around $150 billion or more. Yet, I think the emotional value of the care many women provide their elderly relatives or neighbors cannot be quantified. So, to be clear, this shouldn't be taken as a "why not to provide caregiving" spiel. Instead, it should be seen as a call for "why to *prepare* for caregiving" or "how to lessen the financial and emotional burden of caregiving."

Funding Your Own Retirement

For these reasons, women need to be prepared to fund more of their own retirements. There are several savings options and products, including the spousal 401(k). Unlike a traditional 401(k), where you contribute money to a plan with your employer, a spousal 401(k) is something your spouse sets up on your behalf, so he or she can contribute a portion of the paycheck to your retirement funds. This is something to consider, particularly for families where one spouse has dropped out of the workforce to care for a relative.

Also, if you find yourself in a caregiving role, talk to your employer's human resources department. Some companies have paid leave, special circumstance, or sick leave options you could qualify for, making it easier to cope and helping you stay in the workforce longer.

Saving Money

Women need more money to fund their retirements, period. But this doesn't have to be a significant burden—most of the time, women are better at saving, while usually taking less risk in their portfolios.[64]

---

[64] Maurie Backman. The Motley Fool. March 4, 2021. "A Summary of 20 Years of Research and Statistics on Women in Investing." https://www.fool.com/research/women-in-investing-research/

This gives me reason to believe, as women get more involved in their finances, families will continue to be better-prepared for retirement, both *his* and *hers*.

As I conclude this chapter, I want to leave you with some good news. In the long run, this may be perceived as an advantage for women. Men are more inclined to take risks than women. Taking on too much risk can be a disaster for any woman, or a man, for that matter, as they get closer to retirement or have already retired. A conservative approach to investing later in life—particularly for widows and single women—is understandable and sensible.

CHAPTER 10

Long-Term Care Insurance

Elsewhere in this book, I've outlined the risks longevity poses to your financial health. In fact, you may be tired of hearing it at this point.

Even so, I'd still like to repeat one more time—in case you've forgotten—it's estimated *seven* out of every ten Americans who reach age sixty-five will need long-term care of some kind.[65] Let me ask, if you knew the car you were going to be riding in had a 70 percent chance of having an accident, would you wear your seatbelt?

Long-term care is something to seriously consider in your planning.

I realize there is an enormous expense to maintain long-term care insurance today. But do you think that long-term care cost of care will be lower in the future? Genworth Financial Inc. publishes on its website cost of care by individual states.

Let's look at Massachusetts. In 2021, Genworth estimated that adult day health care cost $1,587 a month. A private, one bedroom in an assisted living facility cost $6,500 a month. And, perhaps not hard to believe, a private room in nursing home care cost $13,535 a month.

According to mass.gov, in 2014, a private pay patient's charge for a stay in a Massachusetts nursing home was approximately $361.77 per day. Although the most recent study estimated that the average

---

[65] LongTermCare.gov. February 18, 2020. "How Much Care Will You Need?" https://acl.gov/ltc/basic-needs/how-much-care-will-you-need

length of stay in a nursing home was 272 days, some stays last for many years. At $361.77 per day, the average annual cost of a nursing home stay exceeds $132,000, but it is not unusual for an individual to pay more than $150,000 per year in some nursing homes.

While costs and services vary from state to state, I include these figures as reference points.

The bottom line is we need to do a better job of planning for the possibility of long-term care. A public poll of Americans recently revealed nearly two-thirds of the public (63 percent) favor more involvement from the federal government to help provide health care coverage for Americans.[66] However, if you think about the current problems plaguing government-run programs such as Social Security, Medicaid, and Medicare, I think it stands to reason, for the time being, we're probably on our own.

Elsewhere, I covered the various ways of preparing for our own possible long-term care costs, from self-funding to insurance riders. I'd like to take a moment to expand on what is one of the most comprehensive coverage options: long-term care insurance.

LTCI Basics

The long-term care insurance, or LTCI, space has had a bit of a shakeup in the past few years. Many insurers stopped offering LTCI, and the policies remaining are often more expensive. In addition, denials of LTCI applications have risen to the point almost one-third of those between sixty and sixty-five are rejected.[67]

Yet, the other side of the coin is the insurers who are left in the LTCI space have experience and policies that have endured. LTCI may be more expensive for individuals, but that's because they can

---

[66] Bradley Jones. Pew Research Center. September 29, 2000. "Increasing share of Americans favor a single government program to provide health care coverage." https://www.pewresearch.org/fact-tank/2020/09/29/increasing-share-of-americans-favor-a-single-government-program-to-provide-health-care-coverage/

[67] Alexander Sammon. The American Prospect. October 20, 2020. "The Collapse of Long-Term Care Insurance." https://prospect.org/familycare/the-collapse-of-long-term-care-insurance/

be more expensive for insurers and because overall long-term care is just plain expensive, period. It's important to understand LTCI carriers aren't just making money hand-over-fist with these products. Instead, the carriers who have stopped selling policies were likely carriers who had unrealistic prices and underperforming policies. Unfortunately, it looks like the current market might only get more expensive in the next few decades.[68]

While many criticize the use-it-or-lose-it nature of LTCI, it is reasonable to consider that homeowner's insurance, car insurance, term life insurance, and many other types of insurance work the same way. Yes, you are paying into a policy in the hopes you may never use it. But, if you must use it, it can provide value well beyond the actual dollars you have paid into it. An average of 358,500 experience a structural home fire every year[69] for the 129.93 million households in the United States,[70] you have *less than a half a percent chance* of experiencing a home fire in any given year. Most of us would still squirm at the thought of not having homeowner's or renter's insurance to cover fire damage, however. Paradoxically, while LongTermCare.gov cites that among those of us turning sixty-five stand a 70 percent chance of needing long-term care,[71] only 7 percent of Americans have LTCI.[72]

To purchase LTCI, you have to complete an application that includes a medical questionnaire. Depending on your age and the insurance carrier, you also may need to complete a medical exam. If

---

[68] American Association for Long-Term Care Insurance. January 12, 2021. "2021 Long Term Care Insurance Price Index Released." https://www.aaltci.org/news/long-term-care-insurance-association-news/2021-long-term-care-insurance-price-index-released-for-age-55
[69] Taylor Covington. thezebra.com. April 28, 2021. "House Fire Statistics and Facts in 2020." https://www.thezebra.com/resources/research/house-fire-statistics
[70] Statista 2021. "Number of households in the U.S. from 1960 to 2021 (in millions)." https://www.statista.com/statistics/183635/number-of-households-in-the-us/
[71] LongTermCare.gov. February 18, 2020. "How Much Care Will You Need?" https://acl.gov/ltc/basic-needs/how-much-care-will-you-need
[72] Alexander Sammon. The American Prospect. October 20, 2020. "The Collapse of Long-Term Care Insurance." https://prospect.org/familycare/the-collapse-of-long-term-care-insurance/

you qualify, then the insurance company will offer you a policy with certain coverage and pricing based in part on your odds of needing long-term care in the future. The younger you are, the more likely you are to qualify—at a rate that is more likely affordable for you.

LTCI premiums count as medical expenses and may potentially be paid with special tax considerations. For instance, if you are eligible to itemize your medical expenses, LTCI premiums can be itemized. Or, alternately, you can pay premiums with tax-free money in health savings accounts. The amount you can withdraw tax-free for LTCI premiums depends on your age.

If you have an LTCI policy, coverage typically will kick in when you have been medically shown to be unable to perform two or more activities of daily living (ADLs). An ADL is an activity such as bathing, toileting, eating, dressing, grooming, etc. These are all things we naturally prefer to do by ourselves; they are markers of our independence and ability to take care of ourselves. Once someone is unable to do some of these things alone, they need long-term help. So, if you have LTCI, once you reach this point you will qualify for a daily amount of coverage over a pre-selected time period, depending on the terms of your policy. That money could be used to cover a nursing home, in-home care, or community organization care. The benefits will begin after the policy's elimination period, which you choose when you purchase the policy. The elimination period can range from 0 to 180 days, and the shorter the elimination period, the higher the premium.

With LTCI, you can pick and choose facilities or care options according to your standards instead of having the government decide what is best for you.

Long-Term Care Partnership Program

One other significant advantage of LTCI is many plans are eligible for a federal-state government initiative called the Long-Term Care

Partnership Program.[73] This program is a joint effort by the federal government and certain states to help individuals decide to choose LTCI protection. It means, if you deplete your LTCI coverage and find yourself in a position of having to spend down your assets to become eligible for Medicaid, part or all of your LTCI coverage limit will extend to your assets. Here's what this might look like "in real life" (using, of course, a completely hypothetical person):

Jennifer chooses an LTCI policy to cover up to three years of nursing home care (a little more than the average long-term care stay) in a semi-private room. After several injuries render her unable to dress or bathe herself, Jennifer moves to Winters Retirement Community. Jennifer is not average. Her policy has paid out more than $250,000 on her behalf, and her policy benefits are now exhausted. This puts her in position for a Medicaid spend down. However, because she purchased a policy her state approved in line with the Long-Term Care Partnership Program, instead of having to spend down her assets to the Medicaid requirement and leaving very little for her family to inherit, she is allowed to set aside $250,000 on top of her state's other spend-down exemptions.

LTCI — It's Not Just About You

Aside from the aforementioned partnership program and possible tax advantages of traditional LTCI, I think perhaps one of the most compelling arguments in favor of preparing for the likelihood of long-term care has less to do with our own personal assets and more to do with others.

What do I mean? Well, I hear from lots of people who think it won't matter. "Oh, by the time I reach the point of needing long-term care, I'll be out of my mind. Who cares who takes care of me and how that happens?"

---

[73] American Association for Long-Term Care Insurance. 2022. "Long Term Care Insurance Partnership Plans." http://www.aaltci.org/long-term-care-insurance/learning-center/long-term-care-insurance-partnership-plans.php

However, like estate planning, long-term care planning isn't solely about us. In fact, I might argue that the most important piece of long-term care planning isn't about you at all. It's about your loved ones. It's about your spouse, your children, or your friends, and how caring for you could impact them if you don't have the necessary resources.

Most caregiving for the elderly happens in people's private homes. A survey of caregivers reveals just a sampling of how a long stint of caring for relatives and loved ones can affect the caregivers:[74]

- Of those surveyed, an average of nineteen hours a week was provided in care. Among those, about 38 percent had to cut back their hours at their job.
- More than half reported that their personal and mental health was impacted, including depression and a lower standard of living.
- 66 percent of caregivers used their personal assets, like savings and retirement funds, to pay for a loved one's care.
- 52 percent of caregivers moved closer to the loved one for whom they provided care.

Because of its benefits for both the policy holder and his or her family or caregiver, LTCI can be a valuable asset in any retirement plan.

*****

Let me take a moment to shift gears and address the larger issue of insurance in general.

The first point I would like to make is about signing up for insurance. We have all been there. Whether it is for a new job or perhaps through a state insurance exchange, we likely have had the opportunity to enroll in a program. For some of us it happens yearly, giving us the chance to make any necessary changes. All too often it

[74] Genworth. November 16, 2021. "Beyond Dollars 2021." https://pro.genworth.com/riiproweb/productinfo/pdf/682801BRO.pdf

is easy to simply check the box at open enrollment without giving things much thought. I encourage you to slow down during that moment when you sign up, and really evaluate the overall value of each plan, choice of providers, and the stability of the company behind each option. Balance these and other considerations with your health history and the money you have spent in the past. This exercise may help you save money while still having adequate coverage.

This brings me to another topic. While this chapter has focused principally on paying for insurance coverage, more specifically, long-term care coverage, you should also consider doing an insurance inventory on all of your coverage, on an annual basis. You may discover that you have too much insurance. I know that sounds counterintuitive and perhaps it is farfetched, but I want to share the following with you.

Recently, we met with a couple who had eleven insurance policies with annual premiums totaling $16,000. Their kids were grown and out of the house, their home was paid off, and they had no debt.

Upon a full review of their financial circumstances, we believed it was hard to justify the expense without an insurable need. They were spending over $1,333 a month just for these policies. Imagine what they could have been spending money on: everyday living expenses, vacation funds, investments, tweaking long-term care insurance, or even spoiling their grandkids. They now had newfound money that could be put to more productive use.

Here is what we discovered in our review process: The couple's polices were set up years in the past and they had, like so many of us are prone to, a "set it and forget it" approach to these policies; payments were automatically deducted from their bank account.

Staggering insurance coverage can be an effective technique as one's needs ebb and flow.

Life insurance is an integral part of your overall financial plan.

*****

Your financial advisor should discuss with you in detail all off your insurance needs and review all of your policies. You should have the right coverage and you should not overpay for the coverage you have—as our clients came to understand.

CHAPTER 11

Finding a Financial Professional

I t doesn't have to be difficult.

On one hand, searching for a financial advisor is easier today than ever before. On the other hand, it can be challenging, given the myriad choices people have at their disposal today to search for, and work with, financial professionals in financial planning.

Still, advances in technology have allowed most people to do their own research. You can peruse websites; you can check with regulatory overseers; you can listen to radio shows, podcasts; you can watch YouTube videos or commercial shows; you can attend sponsored events; you can pursue free consultations; and, finally, you can inquire the old-fashioned way… referrals.

The real question to ask is, "Which firm is the right fit for me?"

Kelly Financial Services has been working with people for 20 years now. Because of this, I think I can share some perspective with you that carries some authority.

Perhaps most importantly, Kelly Financial Services is not for everyone. We don't pretend to be all things to all people. That said, prospective clients for any financial services company—especially in the retirement planning sector—need to ask themselves what attributes they are looking for. In other words, "What are your priorities?" Is it technology? Convenient locations? Frequent meetings? Professional credentials? Processes? Friendly advisors? Maybe a tipping point is fee arrangements?

All of these are valid things to consider. It is a bit of a juggling act to weigh determining your wants and identifying your needs. Not to mention aligning those factors with the service delivery model (features and benefits) of the firm you are considering, too. You also should consider which firm will most likely help you achieve your goals and help you live the kind of lifestyle you desire.

You are probably now realizing that finding a financial professional is not as simple as you thought. But look at this from a higher plane. It might help you sort things out.

At Kelly Financial Services, I am confident that people choose to work with us for three principal reasons: values, trust, and knowledge/capabilities. In that order.

Values

When I consider any long-term relationship, I think the success of it from the beginning rests on a common set of values. For us, that is a starting point.

Bill Kelly was a trailblazer when he started on radio. Obviously, the bulk of the show centered around finance and retirement. But Bill tapped into something powerful. He also openly talked about culture and values. I don't recall too many financial services firms, if any, that were engaging with listeners in this way on financial radio back then—or even today. True, the program included the more-generic "family values" that we all intuitively know about, even if we cannot adequately define them. Yet Bill would talk about who he was: Christian, conservative, capitalist, philanthropist, among others.

He would not shy away from talking about values; he went so far as to promote them, not only defend them. For those listening to him, reading his books, and seeing him in person, they understood where he stood on matters, on both cultural and financial fronts. Collectively, in all of these formats they showcased his values. Many people connected with him and these very concepts. People related to Bill's values and ultimately Kelly Financial's values.

I don't mean to diminish other firms and their clients whose values may be different from our values and those of our clients. That is entirely their right, and I admire many of them.

Nevertheless, my experience has taught me that having a disconnect or imbalance with values between client and service provider can make for a challenging relationship.

I also believe that we view retirement planning a bit differently than many other firms. Retirement planning for us is a value-set unto itself. For instance, it's more than portfolios and pensions. At Kelly Financial, we believe a fulfilling retirement is also about growth in family, friends, and faith. The financial work we do for those in retirement, or planning for retirement—generation, preservation, and distribution of money and assets—really facilitates these noble endeavors. Not the other way around. Our clients feel this way, too.

Trust

I am not a financial advisor (I hold a number of insurance licenses.). When Bill and I started the business, we began in the insurance business. Later, we expanded into managing money and advising clients. As we grew, we made the conscious decision to have Bill run the front office with my role centered on the back office. By the time Bill passed, we had built the advisory side of our business— the front office—so that we had a solid roster of financial advisors on our team. They were instrumental in business continuity during those dark days in 2017. Because of this decision our business was allowed to grow, and we were better positioned to serve our clients. This strategy allowed me to spend more time on business development and manage our external business partnerships, as well as focus on client relationships.

Where does the trust come in? The financial advisors at the firm manage my money. I trust them with my retirement plans. I cannot state it more simply than that. I am a client just as much as I am the head of the firm. And I think people need to hear that.

When a prospective client first contacts our team, we go through an initial consultation that in industry parlance is known as "fact finding." Yes, it involves collecting information, and gaining a better understanding of finances. But I like to view this phase as more of a "trust building" effort. We want to know your concerns, your goals, your lifestyle expectations.

This, too, is a delicate process.

I am reminded of what author Ari Galper reveals with this quote: "Unless, you create a deep trust first any qualification process will make your potential client feel you only want to know if they'll buy your services." He says that building trust is about going down the iceberg with a prospective client. That means having brutally honest conversations with them, going places they don't necessarily want to go. It's about getting clients to open up about their most private selves: their financial selves.

"Going down the iceberg as an advisor," Galper writes, "means helping your potential client understand the gravity of their situation and the implications of not addressing it." Like anything in life, it's how you go about this. Because we embed a sense of values in our business practice, we are confident that this fosters a sense of trust with potential clients right from the get-go.

Knowledge/Capabilities

The financial advice business has come a long way from the days of simply having discussions about insurance products over the family dining table, strewn with mimeographed copies of blurry marketing sheets and signature forms.

The business has evolved even faster in recent years. Not long ago, the advisory business was largely modeled on a bucket of diverse assets that was managed by investment professionals. And success was largely measured by the performance of a portfolio of those assets against certain benchmarks, like the S&P 500. An improvement, for sure, the limitations of this model nonetheless became apparent.

Who cares if you beat the market but are unable to achieve your goals?

Today, the kinds of discussions the advisors at Kelly Financial Services are having with our clients center around goals and lifestyles, not just market returns. It is a better way to get to what is really important to you.

The approach is defined by two key factors: financial planning is *holistic*, and it is a *process*. These two attributes are useful for clients and planners alike. A holistic approach helps identify goals, and a process helps achieve them.

Embracing a process will not guarantee that you will achieve your goals or live a desired lifestyle. But you will have a greater probability of success by using a process. Anyone can hit the bullseye on any given day. You need to consistently hit the target.

Our model better aligns the traditional wealth accumulation, wealth preservation, and wealth distribution sides of our business with financial planning.

We do this with a consultative, team-based model of financial professionals combined with state-of-the-art technology. This helps our clients make better informed decisions. The financial products we utilize are tools to help our clients achieve their goals and live their desired lifestyles. By having a suite of products and services available to us, we can provide customized solutions for you.

I also want to underscore the fact that we are an independent registered investment advisor. We like being independent. We are not beholden to a parent company. Our advisors are not pressured by salespeople to push financial instruments that may not be in the best interests of our clients. We are not hamstrung by being forced to choose from a limited number of proprietary products. We have the freedom and flexibility to work with any third-party service provider we want, all in the interest of serving our clients and their needs. This means a lot.

As the president and CEO of the firm, I have invested in my team, the technology we all use, and the concept of our process. The name of our process ultimately reflects our values and our trust-building foundations. It is called "Safe Money Strategies.™"

The name is derived from Bill. His process—and his entire business approach—was called "Senior Safe Money Strategies.®" When we refined our process and much of our business model, we thought it entirely appropriate to not only pay homage to the past (our roots) but be true to our calling. We dropped the word "senior" from the name because we are now working with the next generation of some of our original clients. We also recognize that the best planning starts earlier—not just when people are older and on the verge of retiring. We encourage people to start as early as possible. It's no longer a "senior only" venture.

Our philosophy today is the same as it has always been. We are fiduciaries, and we take that role very seriously. We do what is in the best interests of our clients. With 20 years of experience behind us, our clients tend to be conservative in temperament and in how they invest their money. Therefore, they steer away from taking unbridled risks.

I am well aware that any investment you make has a degree of risk associated with it—especially with products that are part of the broader financial markets. I look at safety as an approach to investing as much as I do to the outright safety of an individual investment product or investment strategy.

Part of our job is being a coach for our clients. They need to understand our process and understand what we are trying to do for them. They need to be a part of it. If they are not (this speaks to values and trust) then the approach breaks down and risks grow. Clearly, safety from a process standpoint is paramount. Our process helps identify risks in the portfolio and helps people understand what is riskier from what is safer.

After reading this book, I hope you have learned a lot about my firm and me.

Every financial advisor wants to help their clients be better off. At Kelly Financial Services, we're also dedicated to this idea: We want to see them be better, too.

A Matter of Fees

In recent years, advertising in your local newspaper has diminished. So too has the size of the paper. More people are accustomed to reading news online, or look for other sources, including those without a paywall. Advertisers don't find as much value in placing ads in the actual print version of the paper. Declines in circulation are to blame. Also, many former advertisers have company websites, which they use to drive consumer traffic.

However, if you happen to be someone who receives the newspaper in your driveway, you might have noticed that grocery store circulars are still a thing. Sure, the circulars might be a bit smaller. Yet, grocers still see some advantages to listing numerous prices for sales items in print, which readers can often scan much easier than looking up individual items on a website.

Those newspaper ads continue to be printed as a service to consumers. They want to see prices—in some cases before they ever step into the store—so they can prepare their shopping lists accordingly.

Why then should the cost of doing business with a financial professional often seem like a clandestine mystery? Well, to be blunt, it shouldn't. Consumers should know how much it will cost them to work with a financial professional and how exactly they arrive at the fees charged.

Now, fees can be troublesome. You can't get something for nothing, and fees are how many financial companies and professionals make a living. Yet, it's important to recognize even a fee of a single percentage point is money out of your pocket—money that represents not just the one-time fee of today but also represents an opportunity cost. For someone approaching retirement, how much do you think fees may have cost them over their lifetime?

It is important to look at management fees and assess if you think you're getting what you pay for. If you pay 1 percent in fees rather than 0.5 percent over a thirty-year period, you would have to save $2,156 more each year to finish with the same amount of savings in retirement.[75]

While the financial services industry continues to weigh how best to levy clients' fees (and whether subscription or asset under management fee models make for the best approach), firms must contend with how the industry's opacity on fee information makes it harder for clients to understand—and compare—what advisors offer.

Fee models have evolved over time. And going forward, we might see more financial professionals adopt a hybrid fee model. For some clients this might mean a combination of being charged a fee for asset management (usually based on a percentage of the assets being managed) and individual one-time fees or activity fees, such as setting

---

[75] Jean Folger. Investopedia. February 25, 2022. "Lower 401(k) Fees Mean More Money at Retirement." https://www.investopedia.com/how-to-lower-your-401-k-fees-4691479

up a financial plan or a trust. More recently, we are also seeing a newer kind of model. This structure charges clients what is called a subscription-based fee and it is tied to a client's complexity, rather than assets or income.

You should fully understand what you are paying for.

Kelly Financial Services is a fiduciary. We are required to put our clients' interests above our own. And because we are a fiduciary, we have thought long and hard about how we charge our clients for our services. And the same goes for how we compensate our advisors.

First, we disclose our fee arrangements with prospective clients (and clients) as soon as we meet with them. Currently, we charge an asset management fee for most of our clients. But as our business evolves and the needs of each client evolves, it is conceivable that we too embrace a hybrid fee model.

Second, compensation of financial professionals can get very tricky. We have all seen and read about the perverse incentives that can drive salespeople into making decisions on behalf of clients that do not serve the interests of the client. Make no mistake about it, we are not salespeople at Kelly Financial. And we value our independence and our role as a fiduciary.

So to emphasize the point, we don't pay our financial advisors like salespeople. Rather, we pay them with a base salary along with goals-based bonuses. They do not receive commissions on any business they bring to the firm. We believe this helps reinforce the idea of providing the most objective advice we can give to our clients, and this helps eliminate any conflicts of interest, perceived or otherwise.

Acknowledgments

First, to the amazing wives and children who are the backbone of our families, helping us make our lifelong dreams a reality. And to our spouses, who lead us in such a positive way. I know firsthand—Bill Kelly's grit and dedication to our family and Kelly Financial helped shape who we are today.

To our clients, we appreciate so much—it has been through your shared experiences, stories, trials and tribulations, that we have been privileged to work toward your financial independence and desired lifestyle. You have made us a part of your lives and a part of your families, and you have turned to us in good times and bad, allowing us as a company to grow and become a great success in our community. Without your loyalty and faith in us, it would have been impossible to conceive Kelly Financial as an intergenerational institution that it has become, and we would not be able to continue to help people like you every single day.

And last, but certainly not least, to my Kelly Financial team. I am so proud of your dedication, hard work, and persistence on a daily basis. For that, I am deeply appreciative.

About the Author

Kelly Kelly, Kelly Financial Services LLC

Kelly Kelly is president, chief executive officer, and co-founder of Kelly Financial Services LLC.

A native of Georgia, Kelly began her involvement in business early. By age fifteen, she was already doing accounting work for her family's John Deere dealership.

Kelly earned a bachelor's degree in business administration from Valdosta State University. Soon thereafter, she worked for a large marketing services firm that specialized in financial institutions. She also founded and ran a successful gourmet specialty food business for more than ten years.

In 2003, Kelly and her husband, William A. Kelly (Bill), founded Kelly Financial Services. She served as marketing director, built the company's call center and was subsequently named chief operating officer. Upon Bill's sudden passing in late 2017, Kelly became CEO.

Kelly has steadfastly remained committed to the company's mission: helping retirees and pre-retirees to lead a fulfilling lifestyle they desire and deserve. That mission was reinforced by a philosophy that was at the core of the company's founding and remains a guiding principle for Kelly today: financial education serving family values.

Under Kelly's leadership, the company has expanded. It now has a second, fully functional office in Burlington, Massachusetts, to complement the original Braintree location. In addition, she has made upgrades to technology and portfolio management, as well as the service delivery team.

Today, Kelly holds life insurance licenses in Massachusetts, Rhode Island, New Hampshire, Connecticut, Florida, and Arizona.

When not running Kelly Financial, Kelly devotes her time to charitable institutions that she and Bill long supported together. She loves tennis and baseball and, most of all, spending time with her children, William and Mary Madeline.

Made in the USA
Middletown, DE
30 January 2023